Post-Christendom Studies

Volume 5—2020–2021

Contents

STEVEN M. STUDEBAKER AND TAYLOR MURRAY
Christian Outreach in Post-Christendom:
Editor's Introduction — 3

DAVID M. GUSTAFSON
Evangelists of Church History: Wisdom for
Evangelism in Western Contexts Today — 5

MARK ELLINGSEN
What to do About America's Nones — 33

CHERYL M. PETERSON
God's Mission has a Church, but does God's
Mission have a Scripture? — 55

RICK RICHARDSON
From the Will to Power to the Power of Weakness:
Toward a Post-Christendom Evangelism — 76

Modern Authors Index — 109

Senior Editors
Steven M. Studebaker
Lee Beach
Gordon L. Heath

Editorial Assistant: Taylor Murray

Editorial Board

Dr. Najib G. Awad (Hartford Seminary, USA)
Dr. Lee Beach (McMaster Divinity College, Canada)
Dr. John E. Franke (Second Presbyterian Church, Indianapolis, IN, USA)
Dr. Gordon L. Heath (McMaster Divinity College, Canada)
Dr. Steven M. Studebaker (McMaster Divinity College, Canada)
Dr. A. J. Swoboda (George Fox Evangelical Seminary, USA)
Dr. Joel Thiessen (Ambrose University, Canada)

Post-Christendom Studies, a peer-reviewed academic journal produced by the McMaster Divinity College Centre for Post-Christendom Studies (https://pcs.mcmasterdivinity.ca/), publishes research on the nature of Christian identity and mission in the contexts of post-Christendom.

Articles are posted on the McMaster Divinity College website at https://pcs.mcmasterdivinity.ca/pcs-journal, and, at the end of the year, the volume is available in hard copy as well. Manuscripts and communications should be addressed to the Editorial Assistant at mdccpcs@mcmaster.ca.

Copies of the printed version can be ordered from Wipf and Stock Publishers (wipfandstock.com).

Content of *Post-Christendom Studies* is copyright by McMaster Divinity College. For more information about McMaster Divinity College, please visit the College's website at www.mcmasterdivinity.ca.

ISSN 2561-4738
ISBN 978-1-6667-3370-9

CHRISTIAN OUTREACH IN POST-CHRISTENDOM: EDITOR'S INTRODUCTION

Steven M. Studebaker
McMaster Divinity College, Hamilton, ON, Canada

Taylor Murray
McMaster Divinity College, Hamilton, ON, Canada

The term "evangelism" refers to the practice of proclaiming the "good news" of the gospel of Jesus Christ. In post-Christendom, however, it sometimes conjures up images of sandwich-board-wearing, leaflet-handing, street-corner preachers. Due to this perception, in his study *Evangelism after Christendom*, Bryan Stone calls evangelism "the E-word."[1] Even so, as Stuart Murray notes, evangelism remains necessary in post-Christendom, even if it must take new forms. He writes that "opportunities to tell an unfamiliar story will multiply; but old patterns and approaches will seriously hinder our ability to respond."[2] So how should Christians approach this new context? The articles in this edition of *Post-Christendom Studies* seek to offer a few insights on this question.

In the first article, David M. Gustafson draws lessons for today from various evangelists from the history of Christianity. In particular, he looks at Basil of Caesarea, Patrick of Ireland, Proba of Rome, Ansgar of Bremen, August Francke of Halle, Rebecca Protten of St. Thomas, and David Nasmith of Glasgow. Although now we live and minister in post-Christendom, through the lives of these prominent figures, he shows that we should not necessarily abandon every practice from our Christendom past.

Next, Mark Ellingsen turns our attention to the religious "Nones" (those who select "none" when asked for religious

---

1. Stone, *Evangelism after Christendom*, 9.
2. Murray, *Post-Christendom*, 171.

affiliation on national censuses) and argues that churches need to move beyond "business as usual." In order to address this unfamiliar context and reach these individuals, he proposes that believers should approach theology with a scientific method.

Cheryl M. Peterson revisits the idea of the church's mission and poses the question: "Who is God calling us to be?" She suggests that Christians should reframe their understanding of their role in the world as a mission of reconciliation. When viewed in this way, she notes, it is 2 Cor 5:14–21 that serves as a foundational passage for the *missio Dei*.

In the final article, Rick Richardson takes a listening ear to the postmodern criticism of metanarratives in order to gain insight into how Christians can more effectively communicate the Grand Narrative of Scripture in post-Christendom.

Although post-Christendom poses various challenges, it may also provide new opportunities. Each of the articles in this edition of *Post-Christendom Studies* raises questions worth asking in this new context.

Bibliography

Murray, Stuart. *Post-Christendom: Church and Mission in a Strange New World*. 2nd ed. After Christendom Series. Eugene, OR: Cascade, 2018.

Stone, Bryan. *Evangelism after Christendom: The Theology and Practice of Christian Witness*. Grand Rapids: Brazos, 2006.

EVANGELISTS OF CHURCH HISTORY:
WISDOM FOR EVANGELISM IN WESTERN CONTEXTS TODAY

David M. Gustafson
Trinity Evangelical Divinity School, Deerfield, IL, USA

In our Western context, where Christianity is increasingly displaced from its earlier place of prominence and influence, evangelism appears more challenging than ever. If modernism and postmodernism have not been challenging enough, contemporary critical theories have raised suspicions toward evangelical theology and those who seek to evangelize. Christians who hold convictions about the evangel (from Greek, εὐαγγέλιον, *euangélion*) are also confronted with religious pluralism. Moreover, they face a broader secular society with an acceptance of moral alternatives and diversity of sexual expressions and experiences.[1]

Despite challenges, Christians can glean insights from evangelists of church history. Christian practices from past centuries can inform our contemporary understandings and methods of sharing the gospel, even in our late- or post-Christendom contexts. While the history of evangelism is filled with both positive and negative examples, this article sets forth seven evangelists who provide positive examples and give helpful insights as to what may be beneficial to the church's witness today. We will examine Basil of Caesarea, Patrick of Ireland, Proba of Rome, Ansgar of Bremen, August Francke of Halle, Rebecca Protten of St. Thomas, and David Nasmith of Glasgow. Following the examination of the seven examples from history, the essay will present contemporary correlations and applications. Since the evangelists described in this article carried out their ministries during the era of

---

1. Carson, *The Gagging of God*, 18–21, 491–95.

Christendom, we begin with a brief description of developments in the fourth century.

Development of Christendom

In 313, Emperor Constantine met with Emperor Licinius and together they agreed to end the persecution of Christians by signing the Edict of Milan.[2] With this act, Christianity received legal status from the Roman state.[3] In the following years, the church not only enjoyed legal status but Christianity received favorable treatment by Constantine as he enacted legislation to benefit the church.[4] This introduced a new era—the Constantinian era—that brought significant changes to the relationship between church and state.[5]

While Christians benefited from their new legal status, the change also brought negative consequences and dangers. As Christianity became favored by the state, vast numbers of people streamed into Christian congregations. As could be expected, many people identified as Christians because of the civil, social, and political advantages, and not for spiritual or convictional reasons tied to the gospel of Christ.[6] The confluence of the Roman Empire and Christian faith led to what has been described as *corpus Christianum* or Christendom, the "alliance of throne and altar."[7] The alliance became official in 380, under Emperor Theodosius, when he issued an edict mandating Christianity as the authorized religion of the Roman Empire.[8]

---

2. Bettenson and Maunder, eds., *Documents of the Christian Church*, 17; Bainton, *Christianity*, 89.
3. Bettenson and Maunder, eds., *Documents of the Christian Church*, 17.
4. Eusebius, *The Life of Constantine* 1.28–38 (*NPNF* I:494–95).
5. Bainton, *Christianity*, 90–91.
6. Rudnick, *Speaking the Gospel*, 16.
7. Patterson, "Politics," 765.
8. Bettenson and Maunder, eds., *Documents of the Christian Church*, 24. For Augustine's view, see Bainton, *Christianity*, 122–23. The church was to direct the state and the state was to uphold the church. Robert, *Christian Mission*, 18.

During Christendom, evangelism became not merely a matter of preaching the gospel to those unfamiliar with the person and work of Jesus, but a matter of convincing nominal Christians that they needed to be converted to Christ. Often the latter proved more difficult than the former, especially as Christendom became increasingly identified with the Empire, Christian rulers, and majority Roman culture.[9]

Some devout Christians reacted to the influx of nominal Christians into the church by fleeing the church and Roman society altogether.[10] Although they were critical of what they observed and did not want to break fellowship with the broader church, they did so nevertheless for a life of prayer, fasting, and self-denial.[11] By the fourth century, the monastic movement became widely popular, both as an element of protest against the secularization of the church and as a counter-cultural witness to Jesus Christ.[12]

Basil of Caesarea (330–379)

With time, monastic communities began to turn from inward to outward pursuits that included proclaiming the gospel. With this outward movement, monks became the leading evangelistic force of the church. Basil of Caesarea, in the Eastern part of the Roman Empire, led the development.[13]

Basil established a monastery in Pontus of Cappadocia, modern-day Turkey. While he embraced the communal life, his rule for monks turned their lives outward in gospel witness and service to their neighbor.[14] For Basil, the ascetic life of a monk was not to be self-serving but to include gospel witness in word and deed to the wider society.

---

9. Kreider and Kreider, *Worship and Mission after Christendom*, 15.
10. Rudnick, *Speaking the Gospel*, 47, 49–50.
11. Sheridan, "Early Egyptian Monasticism: Ideals and Reality," 15.
12. For a sociological perspective of costly demands of religious groups to mitigate "free-rider" problems that lead to lower levels of member commitment and participation, see Stark, *The Rise of Christianity*, 177.
13. Robert, *Christian Mission*, 25.
14. Chadwick, *The Early Church*, 178–79.

In order to practice this, Basil established a complex of buildings on the outskirts of Caesarea. The complex, known as the *basileas*, contained a home for the poor, a hospital that cared for the sick, a workshop where the poor developed job skills, a storehouse with food supplies, and a hospitality house for travelers.[15] He challenged the rich to remember their obligation to give to the poor, and thereby they would show gratitude to God for all that he had given them.[16]

While Basil was burdened for the poor and sick, he regarded preaching the gospel as the central task of his ministry.[17] He was well-known as a defender of Nicene theology and preached twice a day, expounding the gospel of the Nicene Creed. He praised the earlier work of Gregory Thaumaturgus for bringing the gospel to Cappadocia.[18] Moreover, Basil knew the importance of instructing Christians in the gospel and sending preachers who would reach pagans with the good news. He said:

> The faithful should be instructed in all the precepts of the Lord in the Gospel and also those transmitted to us through the Apostles as well as all that are to be inferred therefrom. . . . That the preacher of the Word should visit all the towns and cities in his charge. . . . That all should be summoned to the hearing of the Gospel, that the Word must be preached with all candor, that the truth must be upheld even at the cost of opposition and persecution of whatever sort, unto death. . . . That we should not preach the Gospel in a spirit of strife or envy, or rivalry with anyone. . . . That one who is entrusted with the preaching of the Gospel should possess nothing more than is strictly necessary for him. . . . That we should instruct our adversaries in forbearance and mildness in the hope of their conversion until the full measure of kindness has been exercised toward them. . . . That we should depart from those who through obstinacy do not receive the Gospel, not allowing ourselves to accept even corporeal necessities from them.[19]

---

15. Smither, *Mission in the Early Church*, 132–39.
16. Rousseau, *Basil of Caesarea*, 136–40. Cf. Holland, *Dominion*, 140–43.
17. Smither, *Mission in the Early Church*, 139.
18. Stark, *The Rise of Christianity*, 37.
19. Basil, *Morals* 70:5, 11, 12, 24, 27, 31, 33.

Basil provided these instructions to prepare Christians for gospel witness. They were instructed in the precepts of the gospel, carried its message to towns and cities, and communicated it in a spirit of peace and patience.

The gospel witness that Basil and the Christian community practiced did not go unnoticed. Emperor Julian, known as "the apostate" (361–363), testified to the charitable acts of Christians.[20] In the spirit of Decius and Diocletian, Julian tried to restore the popularity of Roman paganism.[21] In doing so, however, he recognized that the greatest challenge was the sacrificial love demonstrated by Christians. In a letter to Arsacius, Julian wrote:

> Why then do we [pagans] think that this is sufficient and do not observe how the kindness of Christians to strangers, their care for the burial of their dead, and the sobriety of their lifestyle has done the most to advance their cause? Each of these things, I think, ought really to be practiced by us. For it is disgraceful when . . . the impious Galileans [Christians] support our poor in addition to their own.[22]

Basil's pioneering work to establish Christian benevolent institutions such as homes for the poor, hostels for travelers, and hospitals for the sick, was combined with verbal witness to the story of Jesus Christ and became a common evangelistic practice for centuries.[23]

Patrick of Ireland (389–461)

In the Western part of the Roman Empire, Patrick promoted the monastic movement with his work across Ireland. The number of historical sources about him, including his own *Confessions* (*Confessio*) give details of his life, mission, and theology. While some sources that are attributed to him may not have been written by him, others such as his *Confessions* are without doubt written by him.

---

20. Bainton, *Christianity*, 100.
21. Bettenson and Maunder, eds., *Documents of the Christian Church*, 22.
22. Dickson, *The Best Kept Secret of Christian Mission*, 94; Cf. Stark, *Rise of Christianity*, 83–84, 189.
23. Ferguson, *Church History*, 214.

Before the gospel arrived in Ireland, Celtic islanders were known for their druid culture that revolved around nature, dreams, and spirits. Celtic priests and druids lived in huts or caverns in the forest and professed to know the secrets of astrology, medicine, and arts of divination.[24] Celts were known even to practice human sacrifice and to decapitate their conquered enemies.[25] For these reasons, Romans categorized Celts as "barbarians."[26]

The Christian faith came first to Ireland by Palladius, who in 431, was appointed bishop of Ireland by Celestine, the Bishop of Rome.[27] Palladius's charge from Celestine was not to evangelize the pagan natives but to minister to Roman Christians working in the coastal trading villages. As with later cases, this form of colonial mission was an extension of Christendom, not evangelism among pagans. The ministry of Patrick was different.

Patrick was an Englishman born on the west coast of England in the Romano-British town of Banneventa. His father was a deacon in the local church from the pre-Constantinian tradition, and his grandfather had served as the church's presbyter-pastor.[28] When Patrick was sixteen years old, he was captured by Celtic marauders and transported by boat to Ireland. He was sold as a slave to a man named Miliucc at Connaught near the woods of Foclut. Patrick worked there as a shepherd for six years. During this time, he prayed a hundred prayers a day. According to his writings, he did not value his catechetical training from his youth, admitting that he "cared nothing for religion" and that he was "an atheist from childhood."[29] Nonetheless, his years in captivity changed his views; he became a devoted follower of Jesus Christ.

---

24. Schaff, *History of the Christian Church*, 22–23.
25. Hunter, *The Celtic Way of Evangelism*, 19.
26. Hunter, *The Celtic Way of Evangelism*, 17. In addition to the Celts, the Romans categorized Goths, Visigoths, Vandals, Franks, Frisians, and Huns as barbarians.
27. O'Loughlin, *Discovering Saint Patrick*, 38.
28. O'Loughlin, *Discovering Saint Patrick*, 43.
29. Freeman, *St. Patrick of Ireland*, 13; O'Loughlin, *Discovering Saint Patrick*, 53.

Patrick escaped from his master and traveled to the European continent on a boat carrying Irish hounds.[30] When he returned to England, he hoped never to see Ireland again. However, in a dream, an Irishman named Victoricus came to him with letters from the Irish people. As Patrick read one of the letters, he heard a voice like that of the people of Foclut begging him: "Walk again among us."[31] Patrick tried to forget the dream but when not able to, he concluded that God was calling him to return to the land of his captivity to bring them the gospel.[32]

Patrick prepared for his mission, receiving theological training in Britain, and likely in Gaul because of his ties there with the monasteries of Martin of Tours.[33] After his studies, he was ordained as a presbyter-pastor. In the 432, he returned to Ireland with his "apostolic team," a band of twelve that included priests, seminarians, women, and a brew-master.[34] Although Patrick knew the language and culture of Ireland, he viewed himself as an alien and sojourner among the barbarians.[35]

He and his disciples held open-air meetings where they engaged Celtic people in discourse around the gospel using poetry, story, song, and symbols.[36] He told of a deity greater than those of the druids. He preached the good news of the "God of the three faces" in reference to the Triune God. He preached about this God who provided the sacrifice for the sins of people through his divine Son, in contrast to an angry Celtic god who demanded human sacrifices. Patrick effectively connected revered objects of nature such as trees, fire, and mountains to explain the God of the Bible. He summarized the message of the gospel, saying:

---

30. Bainton, *Christianity*, 128.
31. St. Patrick, *Confessio*, 9.
32. Marshall, "Patrick," 96.
33. Bainton, *Christianity*, 128. John Finney (*Recovering the Past*, 54) says: "It is generally thought that Irish monasticism was imported via Martin of Tours."
34. Hunter, *The Celtic Way of Evangelism*, 21; Mansfield, *The Search for God and Guinness*, 21.
35. Patrick, *Epistola militbus Coroticí*, in O'Loughlin, *Discovering Saint Patrick*, 173.
36. Hunter, *The Celtic Way of Evangelism*, 21, 73–74.

For there is no other God, nor ever was before, nor shall be hereafter, but God the Father, unbegotten and without beginning, in whom all things begun, whose are all things, as we have been taught; and his son Jesus Christ, who manifestly always existed with the Father, before the beginning of time in the spirit with the Father, indescribably begotten before all things, and all things visible and invisible were made by him. He was made man, conquered death and was received into Heaven, to the Father who gave him all power over every name in Heaven and on Earth and in Hell, so that every tongue should confess that Jesus Christ is Lord and God, in whom we believe. And we look to his imminent coming again, the judge of the living and the dead, who will render to each according to his deeds. And he poured out his Holy Spirit on us in abundance, the gift and pledge of immortality, which makes the believers and the obedient into sons of God and co-heirs of Christ who is revealed, and we worship one God in the Trinity of holy name.[37]

In addition to preaching the gospel, Patrick did not hesitate to call on the Triune God to prove himself to the pagan druids. He believed that the power of the gospel must interact with their world and redeem the Celts through Christ at several levels.[38]

When entering a new area, Patrick engaged first with the tribal chief. He knew that if the chief were to convert to Christ, the rest of the tribe would follow. As pagans converted to faith, Patrick and his disciples baptized them. He would then ask the chief or local leader for a plot of land in order to establish a monastery where converts were taught Christian doctrine.[39] Patrick and his disciples then placed the converts in charge of the monastery while he and his disciples moved to an area where the gospel had not yet been preached. Following this pattern, Christians of Ireland were organized around monasteries.[40] These monastic communities

---

37. O'Loughlin, *Discovering Saint Patrick*, 144.
38. Finney, *Recovering the Past*, 87; Gustafson, *Gospel Witness*, 166–68. It is acknowledged that some legends of Patrick in the Celtic church tradition appear embellished.
39. Bainton, *Christianity*, 128.
40. Ferguson, *Church History*, 354; Finney, *Recovering the Past*, 28.

were centers of evangelism, education, and copying of books, particularly the Scriptures and writings of the church fathers.[41]

Celtic Christians were characterized by evangelistic zeal. Like Patrick and his evangelistic band, they believed that every Christian should communicate the gospel with others.[42] One peculiarity of the Celtic monastics was the *peregrinati*, meaning "wanderers," who traveled far and wide.[43] Their zeal led them to function like itinerant evangelists and wandering prophets of earlier centuries.

The ancient document titled *Annals of the Four Masters* reported that Patrick's mission planted around seven hundred churches, ordained about one thousand clergy—both monks and presbyter-priests—and saw the conversion of thirty to forty of Ireland's 150 tribes.[44] According to this pattern, Patrick sought to contextualize his message to listeners while holding to the orthodox teaching of the faith. He worked alongside his evangelistic team who raised up indigenous leaders to multiply Christian communities across Ireland and beyond.

Proba of Rome (c. 352–384)

In another highly contextualized form of evangelism, Faltonia Betitia Proba employed poetry as means of sharing the gospel during the fourth century. After her conversion to Christ, she arranged a type of Latin poem called a *cento* in which she drew from poems of Virgil such as the *Aeneid* and the *Georgics*.[45] Proba's work titled *Concerning the Glory of Christ* (*De laudibus Christi*) selectively used excerpts from Virgil's writings to tell the story of Christ within the Bible's narrative, beginning at creation. In this work, she imbued "the Christ with heroic virtues" akin to the Virgilian hero.[46]

---

41. Schaff, *History of the Christian Church*, 52; Tucker, *From Jerusalem to Irian Jaya*, 41.
42. Ferguson, *Church History*, 354.
43. Finney, *Recovering the Past*, 56–57; Tuttle, *The Story of Evangelism*, 171.
44. Hunter, *The Celtic Way of Evangelism*, 23.
45. Balmer, *Classical Women Poets*, 111.
46. Clark and Hatch, "Jesus as Hero in the Vergilian 'Cento,'" 36.

In a creative and contextual manner, Proba described the events that led to the fall of Eve based on the story of Dido from book IV of the *Aeneid* by Virgil.[47] She employed lines from book II of the same work, specifically about Laocoön's death, in order to describe the words of the serpent in the Garden of Eden. In telling about the birth and crucifixion of Jesus, she selected lines that related originally to Dido and Venus.[48] She wrote: "Because your Son descended from the high heaven and time brought to us with our hopes at last succor and the coming of God whom for the first time a woman bearing the guises and habit of a virgin—marvelous to say—brought forth a child not of our race of blood . . . one with God, the very image of his beloved Sire."[49]

The final section of her poem focused on Christ's ascension and return in glory. Again, Proba conveyed elements of the gospel from the words that originally described the god Mercury and prophecy in the Oracle of Delos, both taken from book III of the Aeneid.[50] She stated her purpose for the *cento*, saying, "But baptised, like the blest, in the Castalian font—I, who in my thirst have drunk libations of the Light—now begin my song: be at my side, Lord, set my thoughts straight, as I tell how Virgil sang the offices of Christ."[51]

Ansgar of Bremen (801–865)

Ansgar—who became known as the "apostle to the north"—was born in Picardy in the diocese of Amiens in northern France, and educated at the abbey of Corbie, a product of Charlemagne's plan to evangelize his empire.[52] In 822, Ansgar was sent with a band of missionaries north to found New Corbie abbey at Westphalia in Germany, and seven years later, he was appointed as a missionary to Scandinavia. Ansgar traveled north knowing that he was

---

47. Cullhed, *Proba the Prophet*, 142, 145.
48. Cullhed, *Proba the Prophet*, 176–83.
49. Liefeld, "Women and Evangelism in the Early Church," 99.
50. Cullhed, *Proba the Prophet*, 185–86.
51. Balmer, *Classical Women Poets*, 113.
52. Rimbert, *Anskar*, 9; Tuttle, *The Story of Evangelism*, 200.

risking his life in an attempt to evangelize the barbaric Norsemen.[53]

Despite any perceived dangers, Ansgar and his assistant Witmar were received and saw Norsemen convert to faith and baptized at the marketplace of Birka on Lake Mälaren, near modern-day Stockholm. Ansgar and Witmar also began a hospital and worked to ransom captives including Christians who had been brought to Sweden from raids and held by Viking chieftains.[54] Ansgar himself purchased Scandinavian slave boys, taking them with him in order to educate them so that they would return to Sweden as missionaries, able to speak the native language.[55]

Beginning with Ansgar, missionary monks in northern Europe used *Biblia pauperum* to communicate the gospel. *Biblia pauperum*—or, in English, "Paupers' Bible"—were collections of graphic illustrations of the life of Christ and corresponding images of prophetic types from the Old Testament.[56] A single volume of *Biblia pauperum* commonly consisted of forty to fifty pages of scriptural images. The biblical illustrations told a story and sometimes contained brief texts. They were designed for common people, especially useful for the vast numbers of illiterate people in northern Europe during the medieval period.[57] Historian N. H. Humphreys stated that *Biblia pauperum* were "popular as a religious work for the instruction of the ignorant . . . the work having been composed by St. Ansgarius [Ansgar], in the beginning of the 9th century."[58] Humphreys further explained:

> It was while occupied in his missionary labours that he [Ansgar] is said to have composed the series of scriptural designs, briefly explained by passages from the Holy Scriptures, which afterwards became known as the Bible of the Poor,—"Biblia Pauperum." In an old copy of the

53. Tucker, *Parade of Faith*, 149.
54. Winroth, *The Age of the Vikings*, 201. When Ansgar arrived in Sweden, Christianity existed there in some form. The church at Kata Gård, a Viking-age farming estate in Varnhem, Sweden, appears to have been founded by a lay lord. Vretemark "Aristocratic Farms and Private Churches," 143–57.
55. Winroth, *The Age of the Vikings*, 110, 203.
56. Melin and Öberg, *Biblia pauperum*, 12–14.
57. Heesen, *The World in a Box*, 65.
58. Humphreys, *A History of the Art of Printing*, 38.

xylographic "Biblia Pauperum" at Florence [Italy], there is an entry, in Latin, in writing in the 15th century, to the effect that the author of the book was St. Ansgar; and this view is further corroborated by several passages in mediæval chronicles to the effect that Saint Ansgarius wrote a book for the conversion of the pagans, entirely composed of signs,—the signs alluded to being no doubt the series of simple outline devices which were afterwards improved into those which served as the models of the first block-book.[59]

These scriptural illustrations were used later to create sculptures at the cathedral of Bremen, and paintings at Hanover, Germany. Bremen became the seat of the combined Bremen and Hamburg archdiocese where Ansgar served as bishop, beginning in 848.[60]

Biblia pauperum were a simple and effective means to communicate the story of Jesus' life, death, and resurrection, and how Jesus fulfilled Old Testament prophecies and biblical images that pointed to him. Each illustration had three scriptural images. The central figure came from an event in the Gospels and was accompanied by two images of Old Testament events that prefigured the central one. For example, the crucifixion of Jesus was associated with Abraham's call to sacrifice Isaac (Gen 22) and Moses lifting up the serpent on a pole in the wilderness (Num 21:4–9).[61] In a second example, the scene of Longinus, the "unnamed Roman soldier" who speared Jesus when hanging dead on the cross (John 19:34), was accompanied by the image of God bringing forth Eve from the side of Adam (Gen 2:21–22) and Moses striking the rock so that water flowed out (Num 20:11). In a third example, the entombment of Christ (Matt 27:59–60) was accompanied by the image of Joseph being let down into the well (Gen 37:21–29), and Jonah being cast into the sea with the great fish (Jonah 1:11–17).

---

59. Humphreys, *A History of the Art of Printing*, 38.
60. Volz, *The Medieval Church*, 43–44.
61. Berjeau, *Biblia pauperum*, 33.

Biblia Pauperum, "Crucifixion, Old Testament," Catalogue of Early German and Flemish Woodcuts, 2 vols (C.1) Willshire 1879–1883. © The Trustees of the British Museum.

Biblia pauperum became an effective means to share the story of the gospel using images. These images of accounts of Jesus' life, death, burial, and resurrection helped listeners to perceive with their eyes while they heard with their ears the good news story. *Biblia pauperum* served as aids for Christians—whether monks, priests, educators, parents, or lay people—to share the gospel more easily and clearly with others.

August Francke of Halle, Germany (1663–1727)

August Hermann Francke was born in Lübeck, Germany, where he was raised by devout Christian parents.[62] At sixteen, he enrolled at the University of Erfurt but then transferred to Kiel. In 1684, he entered the University of Leipzig where he became associated with a group of Christians who shared a desire to know the Bible better, and together they formed a campus society for Bible study and its application to daily life.[63]

Before long Francke became aware of his need for a deeper relationship with Christ. While preparing a lesson on the topic of faith, he experienced conversion, later recalling:

> In great fear I knelt before God on Saturday night and called out to the One whom I yet neither knew nor believed, for rescue from such a miserable state. . . . While I was still on my knees, He [God] suddenly heard me. Then, just as if one were to turn over one's hand, my doubts were all gone. My heart was sealed to the grace of God in Christ Jesus.[64]

Following this experience, Franke's conversion became paradigmatic for others within his pietistic circles. They viewed conversion as a crisis moment or datable event that was preceded by an "agonizing conviction of sin . . . to which one can point for confirmation."[65] From this time, Francke led others to a similar encounter with the grace of God. With promptings by the Holy Spirit, he sought to glorify Christ by "winning souls in every place and by every means possible."[66]

In 1688, Francke launched a full-time ministry to university students. Under this work at Leipzig, students were enthusiastic to read the scriptures, and in so doing, they experienced a spiritual revival that spread to others. As this pietistic awakening gained a large following, opposition came from university administrators who suspended the meetings. At the same time, a friend who

---

62. Olson and Winn, *Reclaiming Pietism*, 51–52.
63. Woodbridge and James, *Church History*, 262.
64. Scharpff, *History of Evangelism*, 29.
65. Woodbridge and James, *Church History*, 2:262.
66. Scharpff, *History of Evangelism*, 29.

served as a pastor in Erfurt asked Francke to come and assist him there.

Francke traveled to Erfurt where he carried out an extensive evangelistic ministry in homes. Whenever he was invited to dinner, before they ate he asked his hosts if he could lead them in a brief Bible study.[67] Despite his work in the parish, Francke soon realized that he preferred ministry with university students.

With a recommendation from Philip Jacob Spener, Francke became Professor of Greek and Oriental Languages at the new University of Halle, founded in 1694.[68] While there, he reoriented the theological faculty toward evangelical pietism by establishing conventicles—small group Bible studies—at the university. Similar to Spener, Francke said:

> Not everyone who calls himself a Christian is a Christian. For a Christian has his name from the Lord Jesus Christ and means as much as one who belongs to Christ, is his faithful disciple, believes in his name from the heart in unfeigned love, even in affliction, imitates him, and is gifted and anointed to that end with his Spirit through whom he is willingly led and controlled.[69]

As for Francke's philosophy of theological education, his objective was to employ "the science of theology," which he posited could "be understood only by means of a lively faith" and in "connection with other means of grace to awaken and advance the Christian life."[70] Moreover, he sought "to establish [students] in the faith and to increase their ability to lead their [future] congregations to Jesus Christ."[71] In order to accomplish these educational goals, Francke not only taught theology in the classroom but lived it before his students by inviting them to join him in his various ministries in Halle.

---

67. Scharpff, *History of Evangelism*, 30.
68. Woodbridge and James, *Church History*, 262.
69. Cited in Sattler, *God's Glory, Neighbor's Good*, 243.
70. Tholuck, *August Hermann Francke*, 464, cited in Taylor, *Exploring Evangelism*, 230.
71. Tholuck, *August Hermann Francke*, 464, cited in Taylor, *Exploring Evangelism*, 230.

They began in the neighborhood of Glaucha, known for its deplorable conditions and economic blight.[72] This part of Halle contained a row of "degrading beer huts and dance houses" that were frequented regularly by people for entertainment. Francke considered Glaucha to be a "den of iniquity" but also a mission field in which to test the transforming power of the gospel.[73] In this neighborhood, he and his students preached the gospel and engaged in discussions in the street and in homes, generally on Saturday nights and Sunday afternoons. His approach was never to preach a message without including the gospel of repentance and forgiveness so that if any hearer heard him once, she could receive salvation. The discussions were based on passages of the Bible or sections of Johann Arndt's *True Christianity*.[74] For a time, Francke distributed bread to the poor every Thursday and invited those who received it to join him for a fifteen-minute gospel message.

Francke and his students met with those who converted to Christ, catechizing them "from house to house" and organizing prayer meetings in homes.[75] Eventually he and his band of student-disciples established a home for Christian single women. Francke purchased a building for the home that had been used previously as a tavern. All of these ministry experiences were spiritually formative, not merely for the newly converted but for Francke's theology students who put their theology into practice.

Francke's experience in the slums of Halle made him aware of the need to provide education to neglected children who did not have opportunities to attend school. After he solicited funds, he started a "citizen's school" for children gathered from the streets. He purchased school supplies and initially used his own study for the classroom.[76] When he discovered that children came from homes that undermined much of what he taught, he began a ministry that furnished living quarters for the students in addition to their education. In 1693, he purchased a house large enough for

---

72. Sattler, *God's Glory, Neighbor's Good*, 38.
73. Taylor, *Exploring Evangelism*, 231.
74. Scharpff, *History of Evangelism*, 30.
75. Taylor, *Exploring Evangelism*, 231.
76. Taylor, *Exploring Evangelism*, 231.

twelve students in which to live. He added another house the following year. In 1698, he launched out by faith and built a larger facility called the "Orphan House" and a year later, he formed the Orphan Latin School for students to prepare them for advanced studies.[77] In 1709, he established a school for sons of nobility, and added a catechetical school associated with the university. His theological students worked with children of the Orphan House, allowing them the chance to practice their newly acquired pastoral skills in the catechizing of children.

Beginning in 1717, despite his other responsibilities, Francke launched an evangelism tour for seven months, holding meetings in cities in central and southern Germany. He preached in churches and homes, and visited numerous public institutions, schools, and orphanages.[78] By 1727, records indicate that in the Latin School there were 400 students, in the citizens' schools for boys and girls, there were 1,724, and in the Orphan House there were 132 residents. The home for single women in Glaucha had eight residents, and a home that he purchased for widows had six.[79] In regard to publishing and distributing books, Francke established the Orphan House Book Establishment that printed and distributed inexpensive Bibles. Editions of the scriptures were not limited to German, however. Testaments and Bibles were printed in Bohemian, Estonian, and Polish.[80]

Despite his work, Francke and his conventicles were criticized for their biblical revivalism and social activism. Even though he was dismissed by the established Lutheran Church for his pietistic views, he received favor with King Frederick William I of Prussia who initiated legislation for similar educational and charitable institutions in his realm. Surely, Francke was a pioneer in university evangelism, small group ministry, and theological education that engaged students in the practice of making disciples.

77. Sattler, *God's Glory, Neighbor's Good*, 59–62.
78. Scharpff, *History of Evangelism*, 30–31.
79. Tholuck, *August Hermann Francke*, 467–68, cited in Taylor, *Exploring Evangelism*, 232.
80. Sattler, *God's Glory, Neighbor's Good*, 84–89.

Rebecca Protten of St. Thomas (1718–1780)

Rebecca Freundlich Protten was born a slave on the Caribbean island of Antigua, the daughter of an African mother and European father.[81] When about six years old, she was kidnapped from Antigua and sold to a plantation owner by the name of Lucas van Beverhout on the island of St. Thomas.[82] She worked for the Beverhout family as a house servant, and learned from them—members of the Dutch Reformed Church—the gospel of Jesus Christ and subsequently converted to faith. At age twelve, shortly after Lucas van Beverhout's death, the family set her free.[83]

In 1736, when more Moravian missionaries arrived to St. Thomas, Rebecca met Friedrich Martin who noted in his diary, "I spoke with a mulatto woman who is very accomplished in the teachings of God. Her name is Rebecca."[84] The Moravian missionaries taught her to how read and write, and involved her in evangelism to the slaves. Despite the hostile environment by slave masters, including violence toward the slaves and verbal abuse toward the missionaries, Rebecca and the Moravian missionaries walked "daily along rugged roads through the hills in the sultry evenings after the slaves had returned from the fields" in order to converse with them about Jesus.[85] For Rebecca, her evangelistic ministry "took her to the slave quarters deep in the island's plantation heartland, where she proclaimed salvation to the domestic servants, cane boilers, weavers, and cotton pickers whose bodies and spirits were strip-mined every day by slavery."[86] Despite the challenges, she shared the gospel with hundreds of slaves, and along with the Moravian missionaries, saw hundreds of slaves convert to faith in Christ.[87]

---

81. Sensbach, *Rebecca's Revival*, 30.
82. Sensbach, *Rebecca's Revival*, 31–32.
83. Sensbach, *Rebecca's Revival*, 25–26, 41–45.
84. McCall, *Aspects of Modern Church History*, 54. Cf. Sensbach, *Rebecca's Revival*, 45–46, 52–53.
85. Sensbach, *Rebecca's Revival*, 3.
86. Sensbach, *Rebecca's Revival*, 3.
87. Woodbridge and James, *Church History*, 459.

In addition to evangelism, Rebecca taught at the church located "at the end of a rugged road through the hills of St. Thomas known to the enslaved as 'The Path.'"[88] In 1738, she and the Moravian missionary Matthäus Freundlich were united in marriage.[89] A few weeks later, Rebecca was named a deaconess of the Moravian community.

In 1742, Rebecca and Matthäus set sail for Germany with their daughter, Anna Maria. Matthäus needed to return to his homeland due to his failing health. Sadly, he died just after arriving to Germany. Rebecca remained at Herrnhut, where two years later her daughter also died. Despite the grief, Rebecca became a respected member of the community and assumed leadership in the Moravian women's ministry.

In 1746, she married Christian Protten, similarly noted for his heritage of an African mother and European father.[90] Eventually, Rebecca and Christian moved to Christiansborg on Africa's Gold Coast in modern-day Ghana, and with the blessing of the Moravian community, taught African children at the Christiansborg Castle School. The children learned not merely how to read and write but the learned the gospel of Jesus Christ.[91]

David Nasmith of Glasgow (1799–1838)

David Nasmith of Glasgow, Scotland helped to found over sixty Christian societies. At age fifteen, he and his friends founded three youth societies that supported foreign missions, tract distribution, and a Bible Society. He began work in manufacturing but hoped to become a missionary, applying to go to Africa and the South Seas, but was rejected because of his lack of education. He then turned his evangelistic zeal toward outlets in Glasgow where he devoted his time to evangelistic and charitable work that included

---

88. Hempton, *The Church in the Long Eighteenth Century*, 85.
89. Sensbach, *Rebecca's Revival*, 102–5.
90. Sensbach, *Rebecca's Revival*, 162.
91. Sensbach, *Rebecca's Revival*, 217–18.

visiting local prisons. He once spent an entire night in a cell with two men who were to be executed the following day.[92]

In 1821, Nasmith became secretary of the Religious Societies of Glasgow. He founded the Young Men's Society for Religious Improvement in 1824, and two years later, founded the Glasgow City Mission that took Thomas Chalmers's district visitation a step further by making the work inter-denominational, enlisting participation from all evangelical churches.[93]

When Nasmith founded the Glasgow City Mission, the society's objective was "to promote the spiritual welfare of the poor of this city, and its neighbourhood, by employing persons of approved piety, and . . . properly qualified to visit the poor in their houses."[94] At the society's first annual meeting, his message to the missionaries was:

> You will convert the houses that [are] tenanted by men of the foulest passions, into churches of the Redeemer, where the Lord the Spirit will dwell and the God of Salvation will be loved and served. You will arrest the progress of vice and promote the interest of virtue. You will make our poor, our ignorant, our degraded population stand forth in all that freshness and fairness of moral and of spiritual excellence.[95]

Besides the Glasgow City Mission, Nasmith formed the Edinburgh City Mission in 1832, and the London City Mission in 1835. With his vision for city missions, he toured Scotland, Ireland, United States, Canada, and France, encouraging local church leaders to form city missions and other evangelistic societies.

Nasmith clearly possessed an ability to organize mission work; however, he was not simply interested in founding mission societies. He stated his conviction plainly, saying, "Every church shall be a missionary body, and every member a missionary."[96] He called churches to awaken from their slumber and to evangelize their neighborhoods. On one occasion, when Nasmith worked in Ireland, he reported:

---

92. Campbell, *Memoirs of David Nasmith*, 57.
93. Shaw, "Thomas Chalmers," 35–36.
94. Burger, *Practical Religion*, 27.
95. Burger, *Practical Religion*, 28.
96. Scharpff, *History of Evangelism*, 94.

Some of the Lord's people here, are speaking of forming a mission church with a pastor, teachers and evangelists; whose object it shall be, not only to edify those who may be associated in church fellowship, but to go forth and preach the gospel and plant churches in the cities, towns, and villages of Ireland, considering that every church is a missionary body. If this is of the Lord, it will prosper; if not, may it come to nought.[97]

In his writings, Nasmith plainly stated that mission societies were merely an "artificial substitute" for the churches of Christ "which are the natural missionary societies, the proper instruments for diffusing the Gospel, both at home and abroad."[98] Nasmith explained further saying:

These societies are of two classes, the natural and the artificial; the former Christian Churches, and the latter voluntary associations of Christian men [and women]. In the order of nature, conventional movements are first, and absolutely necessary. There is no other means of operation in a district of country, or in a locality of a town or city, where churches do not exist, or do not exist in number and strength sufficient to act congregationally upon the population around them. But these [voluntary associations] are only temporary expedients, which must ultimately give place to measures based on other principles. In proportion as churches come to exist in numbers and means adequate to the work of evangelizing their vicinities, the necessity for artificial combinations [voluntary associations] will gradually subside, and may at length be safely dispensed with.[99]

Nasmith's ecclesial view was that "Gospel Churches" should "act on surrounding unbelievers, and at once to absorb the faithful [converts] into their several fellowships."[100] In a letter, written to Mrs. Connell, a relative of Mrs. Nasmith, David reverted to this important principle, saying, "I long for the period, when the churches of Christ, instead of these voluntary associations, formed for this purpose, shall become missionary bodies. There is a

---

97. Campbell, *Memoirs of David Nasmith*, 188–89, 190–91.
98. Campbell, *Memoirs of David Nasmith*, 190–91.
99. Campbell, *Memoirs of David Nasmith*, 449–50.
100. Campbell, *Memoirs of David Nasmith*, 450.

considerable shaking in that respect, in this place, not amongst the churches, but amongst individuals, as to the duty of churches."[101]

Contemporary Applications

Certainly, there are examples of evangelistic ministries of the twentieth- and twenty-first centuries that follow earlier models in church history. For example, Basil of Caesarea's ministry is reflected in the Christian Community Development Association (CCDA) founded in the twentieth century by John Perkins. Patrick of Ireland's practice of "power evangelism" and emphasis on planting Christian communities is seen in John Wimber's emphasis on gospel proclamation with signs and wonders, and church planting as the most effective means of evangelism. Proba of Rome's creative expression of the gospel using poetry is reflected in "Life in 6 Words: The G.O.S.P.E.L." performed by the contemporary Rap artist named Propaganda. Ansgar of Bremen's use of *Biblia pauperum* to explain the gospel within the Bible's redemptive narrative with images is reflected in James Choung's *The Big Story*, using a diagram with four circles to tell the good news of Jesus. Francke of Halle's use of small groups, equipping Christians for gospel-sharing, and publishing evangelistic tools occurred centuries before ministries like InterVarsity Christian Fellowship and Cru that serve on university campuses today. The ministry of Rebecca Protten of St. Thomas to take the gospel to people with little hope was reflected in the work of Consuella York of Chicago who visited Cook County Jail weekly for forty-three years to bring inmates hope through Jesus. David Nasmith of Glasgow spoke more than a century before Lesslie Newbigin about the missionary nature of the church, calling congregations to function as mission societies and for Christians to serve as missionaries in their neighborhoods and cities.[102]

---

101. Campbell, *Memoirs of David Nasmith*, 188–89, 190–91.
102. Guder, ed., *Missional Church*, 4–5.

Conclusion

Our perception of evangelism is shaped by models we have seen. For the past two thousand years, Christians have practiced a variety of means for communicating the good news of Jesus Christ. Examining the evangelism of Basil, Patrick, Proba, Ansgar, Francke, Protten, and Nasmith helps us to expand our perceptions of the evangelistic task that Jesus gave to his church, and to appreciate and learn from their contributions which can shape our gospel witness today.

Bibliography

Bainton, Roland H. *Christianity*. Boston: Houghton Mifflin, 2001.

Balmer, Josephine. *Classical Women Poets*. Newcastle upon Tyne, UK: Bloodaxe, 1996.

Berjeau, Jean Philibert. *Biblia pauperum: Reproduced in Facsimile, from One of the Copies in the British Museum; With an Historical and Bibliographical Introduction*. London: John Russell Smith, 1859.

Bettenson, Henry, and Chris Maunder, eds. *Documents of the Christian Church*. Oxford: Oxford University Press, 2011.

Burger, Delores T. *Practical Religion: David Nasmith and the City Mission Movement, 1799–2000*. Kansas City: Association of Gospel Rescue Missions, 2000.

Campbell, John. *Memoirs of David Nasmith: His Labours and Travels in Great Britain, France, the United States and Canada*. London: J. Snow, 1844.

Carson, D. A. *The Gagging of God: Christianity Confront Pluralism*. Grand Rapids: Zondervan, 1996.

Chadwick, Henry. *The Early Church*. London: Penguin, 1993.

Clark, Elizabeth and Diane Hatch. "Jesus as Hero in the Vergilian 'Cento' of Faltonia Betitia Proba," *Vergilius* 27 (1981) 31–39.

Cullhed, Sigrid Schottenius. *Proba the Prophet: The Christian Virgilian Cento of Faltonia Betitia Proba*. Mnemosyne, Supplements 378. Leiden: Brill, 2015.

Dickson, John. *The Best Kept Secret of Christian Mission*. Grand Rapids: Zondervan, 2010.

Eusebius. *The Life of Constantine*. In *A Select Library of the Nicene and Post-Nicene Fathers of the Christian Church*, Vol. 1, edited by Philip Schaff. 14 Vols. Grand Rapids: Eerdmans, 1979.

Ferguson, Everett. *Church History, Volume One: From Christ to Pre-Reformation*. Grand Rapids: Zondervan, 2005.

Finney, John. *Recovering the Past: Celtic and Roman Mission*. London: Darton, Longman, and Todd, 2011.

Freeman, Phillip. *St. Patrick of Ireland*. New York: Simon & Schuster, 2004.

Guder, Darrell L., ed. *Missional Church: A Vision for the Sending of the Church in North America*. Grand Rapids: Eerdmans, 2009.

Gustafson, David M. *Gospel Witness: Evangelism in Word and Deed*. Grand Rapids: Eerdmans, 2019.

Heesen, Ankete. *The World in a Box: The Story of an Eighteenth-Century Picture Encyclopedia*. Chicago: University of Chicago Press, 2002.

Hempton, David. *The Church in the Long Eighteenth Century*. New York: Tauris, 2011.

Holland, Tom. *Dominion: How the Christian Revolution Remade the World*. New York: Basic Books, 2019.

Humphreys, Henry Noel. *A History of the Art of Printing, from Its Invention to Its Wide-spread Development in the Middle of the Sixteenth Century*. London: B. Quaritch, 1867.

Hunter, George G., III. *The Celtic Way of Evangelism: How Christianity Can Reach the West Again*. Nashville: Abingdon, 2000.

Kreider, Alan, and Eleanor Kreider. *Worship and Mission after Christendom*. Scottdale, PA: Herald Press, 2011.

Liefeld, Walter L. "Women and Evangelism in the Early Church." In *The Study of Evangelism: Exploring a Missional Practice of the Church*, edited by Paul W. Chilcote and Laceye C. Warner, 93–100. Grand Rapids: Eerdmans, 2008.

Mansfield, Stephan. *The Search for God and Guinness*. Nashville: Thomas Nelson, 2009.

Marshall, Caroline T. "Patrick: Missionary to the Irish." In *Great Leaders of the Christian Church*, edited by John D. Woodbridge, 95–98. Chicago: Moody, 1988.

McCall, Malcolm. *Aspects of Modern Church History, 1517–2017: From an African Perspective*. Bloomington, IN: Westbow, 2018.

Melin, Pia Bengtsson, and Christina Sandquist Öberg. *Biblia pauperum (De fattigas Bibel): En Rik Inspirationskälla för Senmedeltiden*. Stockholm: Kungl. Vitterhets historie och antikvitets akademien, 2013.

O'Loughlin, Thomas. *Discovering Saint Patrick*. London: Darton, Longman, and Todd, 2005.

Olson, Roger E., and Christian T. Collins Winn. *Reclaiming Pietism: Retrieving an Evangelical Tradition*. Grand Rapids: Eerdmans, 2015.

Patterson, James A. "Politics." In *Evangelical Dictionary of World Missions*, edited by A. Scott Moreau, 765. Grand Rapids: Baker, 2000.

Rimbert. *Anskar: The Apostle of the North*. Translated by Charles H. Robinson. London: Society for the Propagation of the Gospel in Foreign Parts, 1921.

Robert, Dana. *Christian Mission*. Malden, MA: Wiley-Blackwell 2009.

Rousseau, Philip. *Basil of Caesarea*. Berkeley: University of California Press, 2008.

Rudnick, Milton L. *Speaking the Gospel Through the Ages: A History of Evangelism*. St. Louis: Concordia, 1984.

Sattler, Gary R. *God's Glory, Neighbor's Good: A Brief Introduction to the Life and Writings of August Hermann Francke*. Chicago: Covenant Press, 1982.

Schaff, Philip. *Mediaeval Christianity from Gregory I to Gregory VII A.D. 590–1073: History of the Christian Church*. Vol. 4. Grand Rapids: Eerdmans, 1910.

Scharpff, Paulus. *History of Evangelism: Three Hundred Years of Evangelism in Germany, Great Britain, and the United States of America*. Grand Rapids: Eerdmans, 1966.

Sensbach, Jon F. *Rebecca's Revival: Creating Black Christianity in the Atlantic World*. Cambridge, MA: Harvard University Press, 2005.

Shaw, Ian J. "Thomas Chalmers, David Nasmith, and the Origins of the City Mission Movement." *The Evangelical Quarterly* 76.1 (2004) 31–46.

Sheridan, Mark. "Early Egyptian Monasticism: Ideals and Reality, or: The Shaping of the Monastic Ideal." *Journal for the Canadian Society of Coptic Studies* 7 (2015) 9–24.

Smither, Edward L. *Mission in the Early Church: Themes and Reflections.* Eugene, OR: Cascade, 2014.

Saint Basil. *Saint Basil: Ascetical Works.* Translated by M. Monica Wagner. Washington DC: Catholic University of America, 1962.

St. Patrick. *Confessio.* Grand Rapids: Christian Classics Ethereal Library, 2004.

Stark, Rodney. *The Rise of Christianity: How the Obscure, Marginal Jesus Movement Became the Dominant Religious Force in the Western World in a Few Centuries.* New York: HarperOne, 1997.

Taylor, Mendell. *Exploring Evangelism: History, Methods, Theology.* Kansas City: Nazarene Publishing, 1984.

Tholuck, A. *August Hermann Francke.* New York: F. M. Barton, n.d.

Tucker, Ruth. *From Jerusalem to Irian Jaya.* Grand Rapids: Zondervan, 2004.

———. *Parade of Faith: A Biographical History of the Christian Church.* Grand Rapids: Zondervan, 2015.

Tuttle, Robert G. *The Story of Evangelism: A History of the Witness to the Gospel.* Nashville: Abingdon, 2006.

Volz, Carl A. *The Medieval Church: From the Dawn of the Middle Ages to the Eve of the Reformation*. Nashville: Abingdon, 1997.

Vretemark, Maria. "Aristocratic Farms and Private Churches: The Varnhem Case Study." In *The Buildings of Medieval Reykholt: The Wider Context*, edited by Guðrún Sveinbjarnardóttir and Bergur Þorgeirsson, 143–57. Reykjavik: Snorrastofa and University of Iceland Press, 2017.

Winroth, Anders. *The Age of the Vikings*. Princeton, NJ: Princeton University Press, 2014.

Woodbridge, John D., and Frank A. James, III. *From Pre-Reformation to the Present Day: Church History*, Vol. 2. Grand Rapids: Zondervan, 2013.

What to do About America's Nones

Mark Ellingsen
Interdenominational Theological Center, Atlanta, GA, USA

The marked growth of the Religiously Unaffiliated (the so-called "Nones") in the United States is a well-known fact. The topic made the headlines in the States in 2016 when it was reported that 21 percent of Americans fall in this category. The most recent Pew Research Center study found the number was 26 percent! These are striking statistics, given the fact that in the 1950s only 2 percent of Americans fit in this category, and even in the 1970s it was only descriptive of 10 percent of the population.[1] The situation in Canada is not much different, though perhaps it is a little more dire. A 2018 Pew Research Center survey found that 29 percent of Canadians consider themselves religiously unaffiliated.[2] Of course the situation in Canada is perhaps not as surprising as it is in the United States. We have always assumed that Canada tends to be more secular than the States. These intuitions are confirmed by an earlier 2017 Pew Research study, which found 53 percent of Americans and only 27 percent in Canada report that religion is very important.[3] Given similar levels of Nones in the populations, and despite the aforementioned differences, an analysis of why there is significant growth of the religiously unaffiliated in the States, and what to do about it could have some relevance to and for the Canadian context.

---

1. DeJong, "Protestants Decline," n.p.; Pew Research Center, "In U.S., Decline of Christianity Continues at Rapid Pace," n.p.
2. Lipka, "5 Facts About Religion in Canada," n.p. See Thiessen and Wilkins-Laflamme, *None of the Above*, for similar data based on 2016 polls.
3. Pew Research Center, "Why Do Levels or Religious Observance Vary by Age and Country?" n.p.

In a nutshell, the message of this article is that Christians need to wake up. The Centre for Post-Christendom Studies is correct; we do indeed live in a Post-Christendom ethos. And that means we need new models for Christian outreach. The models that have dominated in European theology and church life for nearly two centuries, and had influence in the States for more than three-quarters of a century (even longer in Canada) are not working. The belief that we can best address secularist trends as Christians by reinterpreting the faith in light of these trends and yearnings effectively trivializes the Christian worldview, makes it just another (not very interesting) option in the marketplace of lifestyle options. The first step in understanding the situation in the States is to come to terms with how it happened and how that has impacted what the Nones believe.

The Religiously Unaffiliated in America: How Come?

Whole books have been written to explain the marked growth of the religiously unaffiliated (in fact, I have just written one myself).[4] Famed sociologist Peter Berger's analysis written 60 years ago remains relevant for our context. This analysis is also in line with the more recent reflections of Canadian philosopher Charles Taylor. Their bottom line is that secularism is a process that makes it plausible not to view all aspects of life as dependent on God. And because we are social creatures, this entails that the process has a subjective side which includes the secularizing of our consciousness. In short, secularization is nothing more than the process of society coming to see belief in God as just one option among many.[5]

A survey of recent American history and a casual consideration of the norms of American pop culture make it apparent that the US (like Canada) has been progressively secularized in this sense since the impact of German Enlightenment thinking on its elite

---

4. See Ellingsen, *Ever Hear of Feuerbach?* Other very different assessments include White, *The Rise of the Nones*; Mercadante, *Belief without Borders*.
5. Berger, *The Sacred Canopy*, esp. pp. 107–8 and Taylor, *A Secular Age*.

universities since World War II.[6] Ever since Immanuel Kant's revolutionary "turn to the subject," scholars in this tradition, among them the founders of the social sciences and critical historiography, have undermined the concept of absolute, descriptive truth in favor of a relativism of values in which everything is equal as long as it is not enforced, and the elite can subjectively create their own values based on their estimate of what is most satisfying or "healthy."[7]

Consider how this philosophy, which also marginalizes religion, undergirds American pop culture today. The iconic Broadway Show, "Hamilton," tells the story of early America without any attention to religion, except when Alexander Hamilton finds therapeutic enrichment in hard times. No mention is made of his grappling with the Christian core of America in *The Federalist Papers* (#69), and James Madison's dialogue with Christian concepts and the faithful throughout the document (#10, #51, #57) is overlooked.

As long ago as when the earliest Baby Boomers were being educated in American schools (the late 1950s and early 1960s) it was possible to learn Colonial American History in public schools and learn nothing of the Pilgrims' religious commitments and how those convictions have impacted life in the New England Colonies or the Constitutional system. The impacts of the Second Great Awakening on the Abolitionist Movement are not subjects in most American History classes (not even at the undergraduate level).

The most watched American television shows of 2020, from police shows like "FBI" and "Chicago PD," to the doctors' shows like "Chicago Med," and reality TV portray images of the good life without reference to religious faith. Worldviews at odds with Christian values make their way into the movies and television and embed in the social psyche, like the comments of Michael Douglas as Gordon Gekko in the 1987 movie "Wall Street":

---

6. For this observation I am indebted to Bloom, *The Closing of the American Mind*, 146–56.

7. Kant, *Critique of Pure Reason*, 41–42; and Herder, *Reflections on the Philosophy of History of Mankind*, 41, 47. For this analysis, see Bloom, *The Closing of the American Mind*, 150–56.

"Greed . . . is good." Journey's 1986 hit "Be Good to Yourself" is a mantra for Americans today. It fits so well the therapeutic ethos which began to saturate the American social psyche along with the values-relativism of the German Enlightenment scholars we have noted. It is a thin line to move from an awareness of our anxiety and the need for counseling in order to facilitate the good life to today's common usage of phrases in America like "identity crisis," "defense mechanisms," "midlife crises," and "burned out."[8]

The therapeutic environment in America counsels individuals to find contentment, to express their feelings, and not to let anything, not even values and binding commitments, get in the way. The special uniqueness of the individual and the validity of his/her unique feelings are prioritized. The media has been promulgating these viewpoints, and all the while the idea of "common sense" embedded in American institutions has taken a hit.[9] Barna Research Group reported in 2017 that 44 percent of Americans regard truth as something felt or relative, and now only 35 percent of us say it is absolute.[10]

The idea that each of us has unique perspectives and tastes is basic to the American (and perhaps Canadian) experience since World War II. The business world is built on these assumptions with its strategies of niche marketing. American business capitalized on cultivating among Baby Boomers their own unique tastes unlike their elders—like Rock and Roll and 60s-lifestyle tastes in drugs, sex, and clothes. Now we niche market to every succeeding generation and group. Less and less, then, do Americans of different ages and backgrounds share common tastes or values. Business and the media thrive on the subjectivism and relativism taught by the academy.[11]

Internet connectivity has played a significant role in further subjectivizing and individualizing American life. For all the praise of connectivity, the COVID-19 pandemic demonstrated what

---

8. Freud, *Inhibitions, Symptoms and Anxiety*; and Freud, *Fragment of an Analysis of a Case of Hysteria*, 77–78.
9. Reid, "Essays on the Intellectual Power of Man," 263; and Reid, "Inquiry into the Human Mind on the Principles of Common Sense," 137–38, 144.
10. Barna Group, *Barna Trends 2018*.
11. For these observations, see Sosnik et al., *Applebee's America*, 160–61.

analysts had been telling us: that life on the internet is isolating and does not make for happiness. Even prior to the pandemic, researchers had noted how use of the internet was invading on personal relationships. People could be seen ignoring their companions or those at mealtime to catch up on the latest internet communication or entertainment opportunity. But heavy use of the internet seems to isolate us from social interaction and the happiness that goes with it in another way. Neurobiologists are noting that excessive use of the internet erodes concentration, and the neurobiology noted in the next paragraph confirms that such excessive use also erodes the parts of the brain which govern such interaction and happiness.[12]

It seems that social connection and happiness are functions of the brain's prefrontal cortex. This part of the brain is its executive function. It keeps in check our animal instincts, the parts of our brain which give rise to fear and fight-or-flight instincts. You need to keep these instincts in check when you are sociable. For friendship you need good manners, not the latest emotions. In addition, nature has wired this executive part of our brain for use, and so we are rewarded when it functions. A pleasant-feeling brain chemical (monoamine) called dopamine is secreted and transmitted to the entire brain. And it seems that dopamine is also associated with sociality.[13]

Since computer usage diminishes these dynamics, it follows that if we use it heavily, we will be inclined toward less sociality, more individualism, and a little less happiness. This is just another example of how our present realities dispose Americans towards evaluating and thinking of everything, including religion, in light of the individual and his or her needs. Heavy computer usage also seems to have a negative impact on our sense of transcendence, as the prefrontal cortex is the part of the brain most active in

---

12. Small et al., "Brain Health Consequences of Digital Technology Use," 179–87; Brad et al., "Prefrontal Control and Internet Addiction," n.p.

13. Carr, *The Shallows*, 116–17, 121–22, 168–69, 213–14, 219–22; Amen, *Change Your Brain, Change Your Life*, 81, 140–41; Immordino-Yang et al., "Neural Correlates of Admiration and Compassion," 8021–26.

spirituality, so diminish use of that part of the brain and you are less open to spirituality.[14]

It is obvious how all the recent cultural strands in America (and throughout much of Western society) have created an ethos making the growth of the Nones possible, if not more likely. The combination of secularism (creating cultural spaces in which religion is just one option among many), customization of products allowing for niches, individualism, and a therapeutic mindset all combine to lead people to hear religious claims as just the articulation of what certain people find good for themselves, proposing a lifestyle option that is not very interesting or not much different than what you can have without it. Now that we have explored how America has gotten to where it is, let us now talk about who the Nones are and what they think.

Who Are the Nones and What Do They Think?

Surveys tell us that if you are a None in America you are most likely a young White male. Polls tell us that 68 percent of America's Nones are White, perhaps as many as 68 percent are male, and nearly 70 percent were born since 1980.[15] Very few are outright atheists (just 31 percent as of 2014) but seem to have some sense of spiritual realities.[16] The optimism about human nature, our essential goodness, and individualism that characterizes much of American society is very much on display in the thinking of the Nones. Human beings need no crutches. We can handle it all ourselves. The Nones generally seek to handle things with a leftward drift, advocating the policies of liberal Democrats.[17] Their

---

14. Newberg et al., *Why God Won't Go Away;* Davidson et al., "Alterations in Brain and Immune Function Produced by Mindfulness Mediation," 121–23.
15. For specific ratios, see Cooper et al., "Exodus," n.p,; Lipka, "A Closer Look at America's Rapidly Growing Religious 'Nones,'" n.p.; Lipka, "10 Facts About Atheists," n.p.
16. Lipka, "A Closer Look at America's Rapidly Growing Religious 'Nones,'" n.p.
17. See Mercadante, *Belief Without Borders,* 132–92; Lipka, "10 facts about atheists," n.p. See Smietana, "Most Americans Admit They're Sinners,"

individualism surfaces in the fact that like most Americans (58 percent) there is a sense among spiritual Nones that worshipping alone or with one's family is as good as regular church worship.[18] A 2017 poll found that Nones are less oriented toward finding meaning in family than Christians and the public in general. Atheists, but not those Nones open to spirituality, may find more value in money and hobbies than Christians and the general public.[19]

We also gain insights about why the Nones became Nones from several surveys. It seems that only 1 in 5 left the Church over a bad worship experience. The biggest reason for leaving religion, they say, is that they just stopped believing (60 percent) but also 32 percent note their family was never religious when they were growing up. Related factors pertain to those raised by divorced parents and in religiously-mixed households are more likely by 10 to 12 percentage points to become Nones.[20] Another statistical characteristic of the Nones, with implications for Christian outreach to them, is that dislike of religious organizations is not high. Only 34 percent of the spiritual but not religious among them have those feelings, according to a 2017 Pew Research Center survey. And in that group only 26 percent find religion irrelevant (79 percent still believe in God) and among agnostic Nones, the numbers are only 40 percent for irrelevancy and 63 percent believing in God.[21]

It is clear that we have some interesting data about the Nones. What are American churches doing about them? What Christian perspective can best address the Nones' worldviews and growth? This article addresses these questions in the following sections.

---

n.p. On the Nones' liberalism, see Connaughton, "Religiously Unaffiliated people more likely than those with a religion to lean left accept homosexuality," n.p.
    18. Weber, "Christian, What Do you Believe?" n.p.
    19. As reported in Lipka, "10 facts about atheists," n.p.
    20. Cooper et al., "Exodus," n.p.
    21. As reported in Pew Research Center, "Why America's 'nones' don't identify with a religion," n.p.

What the American Churches Are [Not] Doing About It:
Business and Theology as Usual

The title of this section succinctly summarizes my thesis. In research for a new book on the subject of this article, I found that mainline American Christianity does not seem visibly concerned about the dynamics of the growth of Nones. It is pretty much business as usual in the mainline denominational headquarters. In a survey of mainline American denominational headquarters that I undertook for my new book, *Ever Hear of Feuerbach? That's Why American and European Christianity Are in Such a Funk!*, I found that none of these denominations has created an office to address the growth of the Nones. It is basically business as usual in these denominational offices, while their resources keep eroding. Granted, there is a lot of talk about the need to make faith more relevant to our situation. But that has been the agenda since the 1960s, even back to the 1950s. It is the rhetoric you use to critique your denominational traditions that you do not like. And it is also true that four of the mainline denominations (Presbyterian Church [USA], The Episcopal Church, Evangelical Lutheran Church in America, and Christian Church [Disciples of Christ]) have developed programs that aim to do evangelism more effectively among the Millennial Generation in ways that are appealing to the Millennial ethos. But these programs continue to trade on the prevailing theological models which have dominated in the American mainline since World War II, if not before.

What is the prevailing theological approach? What American theologian Hans Frei contended in the late 1960s is still most relevant. He wrote: "the story of modern theology . . . has been almost exclusively apologetical, and the main focus has been anthropology."[22] To that he might have added that most of them opt for an optimistic view of human nature, though not of human society (those using Existentialism being perhaps the exception).

It is not surprising that this apologetic model rooted in human experience should dominate in the century or more since the secularization process began to gather steam in Western society. Peter

22. Frei, *Theology & Narrative*, 27.

Berger, in his analysis of secularism, already suggested that what has happened in the churches would happen. He contended that as society gets secularized, so Christianity must be secularized in order to make it attractive to the emerging secularized consciousness, which is effectively posited as a non-negotiable good. As a result, Christian truth becomes consumer-controlled ("anthropological" in Frei's sense).[23] Berger nicely elaborated on the implications of these commitments:

> This means, furthermore that a dynamic element is introduced into the situation, a principle of changeability if not change that is intrinsically inimical to religious traditionalism. In other words, in this situation it becomes increasingly difficult to maintain the traditions as unchanging verity. Instead, the dynamics of consumer preference is introduced into the religious sphere. Religious contents become subjects of "fashion."[24]

In Berger's view, another consequence of the churches' reactions to secularizing trends is that in marketing the gospel it becomes important to focus on its therapeutic value.[25] This clearly harmonizes with why the rooting of religious claims in human consciousness has become the dominant way of doing theology in the West.

Essentially, the secularizing process of which the growth of the Nones is part, seems to have prodded churches into theological models that root faith in human experience, offering a worldview which meets our needs. This commitment was markedly on display in the American mainline churches' reactions to COVID-19—with church leaders not just suggesting but actually *demanding* the cancellation of corporate worship while it was still deemed fine to shop. The call to worship of the Commandments about honoring God or the Sabbath were reinterpreted/ignored in light of the overall demand for health when worship could have been often conducted safely out of doors. Of course, with a theological perspective that lets the culture and its passion for individualism set the agenda (polls indicate that a majority of American adults

---

23. Berger, *The Sacred Canopy*, 147–48.
24. Berger, *The Sacred Canopy*, 145–46.
25. Berger, *The Sacred Canopy*, 147.

[58 percent] believe that worshiping alone or with one's family is a valid replacement for regularly attending church, and only 30 percent disagree) church leaders have plenty of cover for their directives.[26] No matter if such advice was not heeded in the Church's tradition by the Martyrs (who certainly did not prioritize health) or if there will be long-term consequences for losing members or nurturing young people who now know that corporate worship is optional.

When you operate in these ways, and let influential worldviews set the agenda for faith, the transcendence or Otherness of God and faith, along with their call for absolute submission, get lost. And when you do that you miss the warning of sociologist Phil Zuckerman when he observes that if something is "religious" it has to preserve elements of the transcendence, of the supernatural.[27] Lose transcendence and you do not have religion, he seems to claim. Is that the problem we face today: that the dominant strands of theology are not religious enough to appeal to the Nones and others caught up in secularism? Is the problem that the Church is not really offering an alternative to secularism, but just less interesting secular options?

This is where the nineteenth-century German philosopher Ludwig Feuerbach is relevant. His claim that religion is nothing more than human experience is the way most modern secularists and the Nones in particular hear Christian teaching.[28] And if the Church cannot present a version of Christianity that can avoid that conclusion, any outreach to the Nones will not stand a chance of genuinely engaging them. Faith is not something worthy of attention for the Nones. It is just somebody else's opinion, from their point of view. If Christianity is going to get a hearing in our context, in which most everyone hears Christian claims in terms of Feuerbachian presuppositions about them being nothing more than

---

26. Weber, "Christian, What Do you Believe?" n.p. I do not question the good intentions of the mainline church leaders in the United States who made live corporate worship optional, but their well-intentioned directives and actions have been unwittingly conditioned by their propensity to let the cultural winds shape their ministries.

27. Zuckerman, *Society Without God*, 191.

28. Feuerbach, *The Essence of Christianity*, 14.

human wish-fulfillment, then such Christian affirmations must be able to stand as authoritative claims on people's lives, in order to be a real alternative to our feel-good individualism. We need to become aware that our experience leaves us in want, that it is not all there is to life (that we live in a flawed sinful condition), in order to have a sense of transcendence and our need for it. These conclusions seem borne out by the very fact that theologically-conservative churches that do not root faith in human experience like their mainline cousins do (I refer here to the Evangelical Movement, churches of the Southern Hemisphere, the Black church in America) have not taken membership hits like the mainline churches have.

Theology for a New Outreach

What does an attractive alternative look like? Not surprisingly, if we need to endorse a theological position that affirms divine transcendence and does not root the Word of God in human experience, the model for outreach that I propose looks a little like Karl Barth's approach and the Postliberal, Biblical Narrative Theology of some of his followers in the late-twentieth century at Yale University.[29] All of these approaches assert, with Evangelicals and the Black church, that the Word of God stands over against the individual. The Word has authority in my proposal and the Black church's hermeneutical traditions because it does not just tell us about God and Jesus Christ. We actually encounter him in the Word, like you really encounter the missing loved one in telling good stories about him or her. On these grounds, the Word of God does not depend on being rooted in some foundational principle or experience for its credibility. Human experience is not all that good; it is flawed. It cannot be the basis for experiencing God. Such a theological perspective must face challenges to its credibility. How do we avoid the scepter of a fundamentalistic biblicism or blind fideism?

---

29. Barth, "An Introductory Essay," x–xxxii; Frei, *Theology & Narrative*; and Lindbeck, *The Nature of Doctrine*.

The lesson that Barth teaches us is the reminder that theology is a science. Of course, it does not conform to the measurement of other sciences. But it functions like a science.[30] This appeal to its scientific character is more likely to get attention in our secular ethos. Because for all our relativism and subjectivism, secularists tend to defer to science, giving it a privileged role in deciding factual questions. Consider the trust that the American educational establishment has placed in science with its insistence on prioritizing STEM courses (science, technology, engineering, and math).[31] Theology as science makes more sense in our ethos than theology as psychology or some other formula.

In making this claim we need to be sure we understand what scientists today say science is. Science, especially in the field of Quantum Mechanics, recognizes that it does not and cannot have all the answers. No less an eminent geneticist than Francis Collins has contended that science recognizes that it is limited to its own sphere of investigation. It does not provide a full-blown worldview. The quantum physicist focuses on the internal makeup of the atom and is not working with the human brain like a neurobiologist is. But of course, there can be an overlap of interests and findings from time to time. Likewise, science in general is concerned with the dynamics of what is happening, but is less equipped to answer questions of their meaning or why they happened.[32] This opens the door on scientific grounds in principle to allow for aesthetic and religious truths. The claims of the Bible might be true, even if not strictly speaking biologically or historically verifiable. And yet there can be an overlap of interests at times, such that we can speak of faith having scientific or historical implications.

How then can theology operate as a science? In the strict sense of being a physical science, it is not one. But it might be and has been conducted in such a way as to operate scientifically. How does science operate? No less eminent a scientist than Stephen

30. Barth, *Church Dogmatics*, I/1:1–9.
31. Boghossian, *Fear of Knowledge*, 4; Deneen, *Why Liberalism Failed*, 13–16, 91–109; and Wilson, *Consilience*.
32. Giberson and Collins, *The Language of Science and Faith*, 107–8.

Hawking and many others have observed that our old thinking of science as a discipline, which inductively and empirically proves theories, is off base. Rather, certain formal agreements or paradigms guide research and study of data. In that sense, they emerge prior to "proof," though data observed informally may suggest them from the start. Like the atomic theory, for example, or the theory of gravity, these paradigms continue to be presupposed until they can no longer account for new data or support research.[33] In short, the scientific method does not so much "prove" theories as it disproves incorrect ones. In order to be true, a claim must be testable, capable of disproof.

Karl Barth and his heirs who reject rooting faith in some foundational human experiences propose theological models that are in principle scientific in these ways. It is committed to testing its language in relation to the Word of God, and its research is accountable only to this paradigm. Likewise, theories about atoms and molecules as strings set the agenda for research in physics and the research data is interpreted in light of these paradigms. Actually, just as sight is not a valid criterion for determining the existence of molecules in Quantum Physics and their string-like character in String Theory, so visibility or lack of it is irrelevant for determining the truth of Christian claims about God or Jesus' miracles. All sciences, including theology, are in Barth's words "accountable for this path to itself" and "it cannot at the same time take over the obligation to submit to measurement by the canons valid for other sciences."[34] An important American proponent of Barth's, Robert Jenson, claimed that

> We must summon the audacity to say that modernity's scientific/metaphysical metanarrative . . . is not the encompassing story within which all other accounts of reality within which all other accounts of reality must establish their places, or be discredited by failing to find one. It is instead a brutal abstraction from reality. . . . It is time for the church simply to reply: . . . the tale told by Scripture is too comprehensive to find place within so drastically curtailed a vision of the facts. Indeed

---

33. Hawking and Mlodinow, *The Grand Design*, 46, 172; cf. Kuhn, *The Structure of Scientific Revolutions*, 9–10, 36–110, 145.
34. Barth, *Church Dogmatics* I/1:7, 9.

the gospel story cannot fit within *any* other would-be meta-narrative because it is itself the only true metanarrative—or it is altogether false.[35]

Theology, like any scientific discipline, determines its own agenda and standards of truth in the discipline. The truth of a scientific discipline is not found in the beauty of its equations, but in its logic and correspondence with data. (Of course, we can refer to a mathematical beauty of the equations and dialogue can transpire with an artist about whether they are in fact beautiful.) So, likewise, the truth of Christian faith is not found in its correspondence to the theory of evolution or even in many cases its historicity by the canons of historical criticism, but in its ability to represent the biblical witness. (Of course, there may be times when a dialogue with a scientist about compatibility between the resurrection accounts and historical facts is appropriate.)

Jenson's last point, also made by some of the Postliberal theologians, is essential for establishing the scientific character of theology. Theology is not a science if all truth is only internal to the discipline. A discipline is not scientific if it cannot be falsified by testing.[36] For example, in order to be scientific, a theological model like I and my allies propose must be open to being discredited if evidence could be found to demonstrate that Jesus did not in fact rise from the dead (as 1 Cor 15:17 testifies). Adherence to the biblical witness demands that the Christian claim about Jesus' Resurrection be falsifiable. Likewise, since the Word of God functions to absorb our world (what Jenson calls the metanarrative into which everything else in life fits), if Christian faith could be shown to not effectively form our lives, to help people live effectively and well, that might count as evidence against its truth. But in the interim, in view of how well things have worked out for societies in which Christendom was established, in view of poll data indicating regular worshippers are happier than the general public,

---

35. Jenson, *Canon and Creed*, 120.
36. Frei, *The Identity of Jesus Christ*, 138; Lindbeck, *The Nature of Doctrine*, 118, 165.

barring the production of counter-evidence, could a case be made for continuing to posit the truth of Christianity?[37]

The theological model I have been describing clearly presents Christian faith in a credible way as a genuine alternative to the secularized consciousness of the Nones. It almost presents a counter-cultural vision compared to modern American/Western culture. Everything in the world of the Nones points towards solitude, individuality, flexibility, optimism about what we can accomplish, and is about self-fulfillment and well-being. While the gospel on this model offers real-life community and community gatherings (unless your concern about health keeps you away), a life of sacrifice and cross-bearing, a life of continuity with the broader historic community, and a sense of belonging. Accompanied by a strong sense of human sinfulness because we cannot trust ourselves, the theological model I propose claims that the Word of God subsumes our world and experience to it, positing a transcendent vision of God, not subsumed to our experience. Contrary to the optimism of the Nones, this is a worldview that gets us away from ourselves to focus on transcendence, a real counter-cultural option.

The authority of such a Word almost recreates a kind of Christendom ethos which secularism seeks to undermine. It seems to nurture and endorse the kind of community solidarity which Christendom affords for Christian faith to thrive (at least a theological model which can help nurture among the faithful something like Christendom in small communities). As for the attractiveness of such counter-cultural aspects of this theological model, the sense in which it is a contradiction of the values in which the Nones were nurtured, it is worth noting that the Church seems to have functioned most effectively in history when it offered an alternative to the values dominating in high culture. Consider the period of the Martyrs, the Great Awakenings, the Black church in America, the Confessing Church in World War II-era Germany, the church in Eastern Europe in the 1960s through the 1980s, and the marked growth of the church in the Southern Hemisphere

---

37. As reported in *Pew Forum*, "Religion's Relationship to Happiness, Civic Engagement and Health Around the World," n.p.

since World War II. What is counter-cultural gets noted, and polls suggest that there is an attitude in today's American youth about "not caring what they [the establishment] think" which will make a counter-cultural version of the Christian faith most attractive.[38]

You cannot have this thumbs-down to the establishment version of faith, and you cannot present Christianity as a real alternative to our times, without a model of theology which is not heard as just another version of meeting human needs. A theology presented as a credible science, as offering authoritative facts in the discipline like I am suggesting in this article, has a better chance to offer effective outreach to the Nones and their friends than the failed prevailing alternative.[39]

Conclusion

I hasten to add that I am not so naïve as to think that proposing a theology that operates like a science is going to solve all our problems, restore Christendom, and "rescue" or "save" the Nones. Even if I am correct in my analyses, the church (at least in America) will still need to do the sort of things that Rick Warren and other mega-church leaders learned from management consultant Peter Drucker—make gut-level connections, lead with authenticity and adaptability, engage in niche marketing, and nurture a sense of community and small groups with authentic navigators. There will also be a need to develop a rich array of programs in churches which are fun and enriching, perhaps those that target or give more responsibility to Millennials, as some researchers advise.[40] But the more we can get the theological model presented in this article embedded in the pulpits and denominational offices of America's churches, the less the kind of megachurch, successful business strategies just sketched will be needed. Americans (and Canadians) caught up in the world of the Bible and its authoritative Word,

---

38. For this sort of social analysis, see Twenge, *Generation Me*, 17–43.
39. For a fuller development of my theological model, see my *Ever Hear of Feuerbach?*; *A Common Sense Theology*; and "The Future of Evangelical Catholic Lutheran Witness," n.p.
40. Drucker, "Management Paradigms," n.p.

not hung up on whether it is relevant or not, are usually the most engaged and loyal followers of Christ, joyfully serving without any gimmicks. The theological model I have sketched to reach out to the Nones aims to increase the number of those caught up in the authority of the Word and meeting our Lord there.

Bibliography

Amen, Daniel. *Change Your Brain, Change Your Life*. New York: Three Rivers, 1998.

Barna Group. *Barna Trends 2018: The Truth about a Post-Truth Society*. Grand Rapids: Baker, 2017.

Barth, Karl. "An Introductory Essay." In *The Essence of Christianity*, by Ludwig Feuerbach, x–xxxii. Translated by George Eliot. New York: Harper & Row, 1957.

———. *Church Dogmatics*. Vol. I/1. Translated by G. T. Thomson. Edinburgh: T&T Clark, 1936.

Berger, Peter. *The Sacred Canopy: Elements of the Sociological Theory of Religion*. Garden City, NY: Doubleday, 1969.

Bloom, Allan. *The Closing of the American Mind: How Higher Education Has Failed Democracy and Impoverished the Souls of Today's Students*. New York: Simon and Schuster, 1987.

Boghossian, Paul. *Fear of Knowledge: Against Relativism and Constructivism*. Oxford: Clarendon, 2006.

Brad, Matthias, et al. "Prefrontal Control and Internet Addiction: A Theoretical Model and Review of Neuropsychological and Neuroimaging Findings." *Frontiers in Human Neuroscience*, 27 May 2014. Online: https://www.frontiersin.org/articles/10.3389/fnhum.2014.00375/full.

Carr, Nicholas G. *The Shallows: What the Internet is Doing to Our Brains*. New York: W. W. Norton, 2010.

Connaughton, Aidan. "Religiously Unaffiliated People More Likely Than Those with a Religion to Lean Left, Accept Homosexuality." *Pew Research Center*, 28 September 2020. Online: https://www.pewresearch.org/fact-tank/2020/09/28/religiously-unaffiliated-people-more-likely-than-those-with-a-religion-to-lean-left-accept-homosexuality/.

Cooper, Betsy, et al. "Exodus: Why Americans are Leaving Religion—and Why They're Unlikely to Come Back." *Public Research Institute*, 22 September 2016. Online: https://www.prri.org/research/prri-rns-poll-nones-atheist-leaving-religion/.

Davidson, Richard, et al. "Alterations in Brain and Immune Function Produced by Mindfulness Meditation." *Psychosomatic Medicine* 65 (2003) 564–70.

DeJong, Allison. "Protestants Decline, More Have No Religion in a Sharply Shifting Religious Landscape (Poll)." *ABC News*, 10 May 2018. Online: https://abcnews.go.com/Politics/protestants-decline-religion-sharply-shifting-religious-landscape-poll/story?id=54995663.

Deneen, Patrick J. *Why Liberalism Failed*. New Haven, CT: Yale University Press, 2018.

Drucker, Peter. "Management Paradigms." *Forbes*, 13 December 2004.

Ellingsen, Mark. *A Common Sense Theology: The Bible, Faith, and American Society*. Macon, GA: Mercer University Press, 1995.

———. *Ever Hear of Feuerbach? That's Why American and European Christianity Are in Such a Funk!* Eugene, OR: Cascade, 2020.

———. "The Future of Evangelical Catholic Lutheran Witness." *Lutheran Forum*, Fall 2020. Online: www.lutheranforum.com.

Feuerbach, Ludwig. *The Essence of Christianity*. Translated by George Eliot. New York: Harper & Row, 1957.

Frei, Hans. *The Identity of Jesus Christ*. Philadelphia: Fortress, 1975.

———. *Theology & Narrative: Selected Essays*, edited by George Hunsinger and William C. Placher. New York: Oxford University Press, 1993.

Freud, Sigmund. *Fragment of an Analysis of a Case of Hysteria: Standard Edition*. Vol. 7. London: Hogarth, 1953.

———. *Inhibitions, Symptoms and Anxiety: Standard Edition* Vol. 20. London: Hogarth, 1959.

Giberson, Karl, and Francis Collins. *The Language of Science and Faith*. Downers Grove, IL: IVP, 2011.

Hawking, Stephen, and Leonard Mlodinow. *The Grand Design*. New York: Bantam, 2012.

Herder, Johann Gottfried. *Reflections on the Philosophy of History of Mankind*, edited by Frank Manuel. Chicago: University of Chicago Press, 1968.

Immordino-Yang, Mary Helen, et al. "Neural Correlates of Admiration and Compassion." *Proceedings of the National Academy of Sciences* 106.19 (2009) 8021–26.

Jenson, Robert W. *Canon and Creed.* Louisville: John Knox, 2010.

Kant, Immanuel. *Critique of Pure Reason.* Translated by Norman K. Smith. Toronto: Macmillan, 1929.

Kuhn, Thomas. *The Structure of Scientific Revolutions.* 2nd ed. New York: New American Library, 1970.

Lindbeck, George. *The Nature of Doctrine: Religion and Theology in a Postliberal Age.* Philadelphia: Westminster, 1984.

Lipka, Michael. "5 Facts About Religion in Canada." Pew Research Center, 1 July 2019. Online: https://www.pewresearch.org/fact-tank/2019/07/01/5-facts-about-religion-in-canada/

———. "10 Facts About Atheists." Pew Research Center, 6 December 2019. Online: https://www,pewresearch.org/fact/tank/2019/12/06/10-facts-about-atheists/.

———. "A closer look at America's rapidly growing religious 'nones.'" *Pew Research Center*, 13 May 2015. Online: https://www.pewresearch.org/fact/tank/2015/05.a-closer-look-at-americas-rapidly-growing-religious-nones/.

Mercadante, Linda. *Belief Without Borders: Inside the Minds of the Spiritual but not Religious.* New York: Oxford University Press, 2014.

Newberg, Andrew et al. *Why God Won't Go Away: Brain Science and the Biology of Belief.* New York: Ballantine, 2002.

Pew Forum. "Religion's Relationship to Happiness, Civic Engagement and Health Around the World." 31 January 2019. Online: www.pewform.org/2019/01/31/religiouns-relationship-to-happiness-civic-engagement-17-21and-health-around-the-world-/.

Pew Research Center. "In U.S., Decline of Christianity Continues at Rapid Pace." 17 October 2019. Online: https://www.pewforum.org/2019/10/17/in-u-s-decline-of-christianity-continues-at-rapid-pace/.

———. "Why America's 'Nones' Don't Identify With a Religion." 8 August 2018. Online: https://www.pewresearch.org/fact-tank/2018/08/08/why-americas-nones-dont-identify-with-a-religion/.

———. "Why do Levels or Religious Observance Vary by Age and Country?" 13 June 2018. Online: https://www.pewforum.org/2018/06/13/why-do-levels-of-religious-observance-vary-by-age-and-country.

Reid, Thomas. "Essays on the Intellectual Power of Man." In *The Works of Thomas Reid, D.D.*, 1:215–510. 7th ed. Edinburgh: Maclachlon and Stewart, 1872.

———. "Inquiry into the Human Mind on the Principles of Common Sense." In *The Works of Thomas Reid, D.D.*, 1:95–214. 7th ed. Edinburgh: Maclachlon and Stewart, 1872.

Small, Gary W., et al. "Brain Health Consequences of Digital Technology Use." *Dialogues in Clinical Neuroscience* (2020) 179 87.

Smietana, Bob. "Most Americans Admit They're Sinners." *LifeWay Research*, 15 August 2017. Online: https://lifewayresearch.com/2017/08/15/most-americans-admit-theyre-sinners/.

Sosnik, Daniel B., et al. *Applebee's America*. New York and London: Simon & Schuster, 2006.

Taylor, Charles. *A Secular Age*. Cambridge: Harvard University Press, 2007.

Thiessen, Joel, and Sarah Wilkins-LaFlamme. *None of the Above: Nonreligious Identity in the United States and Canada.* New York: New York University Press, 2020

Twenge, Jean. *Generation Me: Why Today's Young Americans Are More Confident, Assertive, Entitled—and More Miserable Than Ever Before.* New York: Free Press, 2006.

Weber, Jeremy. "Christian, What Do you Believe? Probably a Heresy About Jesus." *Christianity Today*, 16 October 2018.

Wilson, Edward O. *Consilience: The Unity of Knowledge.* New York: Alfred A. Knopf, 1998.

White, James E. *The Rise of the Nones: Understanding and Reaching the Religiously Unaffiliated.* Grand Rapids: Baker, 2014.

Zuckerman, Phil. *Society without God.* 2nd ed. New York: New York University Press, 2020.

GOD'S MISSION HAS A CHURCH, BUT DOES GOD'S MISSION HAVE A SCRIPTURE?

Cheryl M. Peterson
Trinity Lutheran Seminary at Capital University, Columbus, OH, USA

Introduction

The Reformers believed that Scripture alone (*sola scriptura*) provided the basis for both our knowledge of God's saving action in Jesus Christ and the means by which God saves. This *sola* should not be separated from the other *solas*: *sola gratia* (grace alone), *sola Christus* (Christ alone), and *sola fide* (faith alone). For Martin Luther, the center or heart of Scripture is found in the gospel of justification, which he found expressed most clearly in Paul's Epistles to the Romans and Galatians: that believers are saved by God's grace through faith on account of Christ, apart from works of the law. As Rom 1:16, one of the most frequently cited Scripture passages in the Lutheran Confessions, states: "For I am not ashamed of the gospel; it is the power of God for salvation to everyone who has faith, to the Jew first and also to the Greek."

As heirs to the Reformation tradition in a post-Christendom context, it behooves Lutherans to go beyond the scriptural basis of the content of the gospel to explore a scriptural basis for the church's mission to *share* that gospel. The question guiding this essay is this: What scriptural passages could—and should—ground the church's understanding of *mission*? First, I address the charge that the Lutheran tradition historically has a "missionary deficiency." Second, I review the concept of the *missio Dei* and its contribution to contemporary theology of mission in a post-Christendom context. Third, I evaluate the "classic" missionary text, the so-called "Great Commission" in Matt 28:18–20, and propose a different foundational text. Finally, I conclude with an examination on the "commissioning" texts in the four New Testament Gospels in light of the previous inquiry.

The Missionary Deficiency of the Reformation?

Many missiologists critique Lutherans for their missionary deficiency, following the assessment of Gustav Warneck, often called the father of mission studies.[1] Warneck charged Martin Luther with a lack of missionary awareness or concern, as Luther did not support a "regular sending of messengers to non-Christian nations, with the view of Christianizing them."[2] Subsequent scholarship has explored why this was the case. Some posited that the Reformers believed that the Great Commission to spread the gospel to "all nations" had already been fulfilled by the original apostles and therefore did not apply to later generations of Christians. Luther himself is inconsistent on this point; in some of his writings he indicates that the gospel has not yet reached the whole world, and in other writings he speaks as if it has.[3] However, as Werner Elert points out, "When Luther sometimes speaks as though the Gospel has already fulfilled its mission in all nations—which has been cited again and again as proof of his lack of understanding of the idea of missions—for him this is the simply conclusion draw from the universal validity of the gospel."[4] It is true that the Reformers had no regular contact with non-Christian peoples, living under Christendom as they did. One scholar points out that Luther likely met two dozen unbaptized people his whole life.[5]

Other scholars have suggested it is unfair to judge Luther by nineteenth-century standards. According to Swedish missiologist Ingemar Oberg, many researchers display an "anachronistic blindness" in this regard. They do not realize how difficult it would have been for Luther and his followers to start a foreign mission. This was due not only to the expansion of Islam, which limited

---

1. Van Neste, "The Mangled Narrative," 1–7.
2. Cited in Scherer, "Luther and Mission," 1.
3. For examples of sermons where Luther makes reference to the gospel not yet reaching the whole world, see Van Neste, "The Mangled Narrative," 11.
4. Elert, "Luther and 'Mission,'" 26.
5. Kolb, "Foreword," vii.

missions geographically, but also because Luther did not have the protection of the Protestant "empires" nor the benefit of laws providing religious freedom in mission lands.[6] Warneck's definition of mission was not only anachronistic; it was also narrow. It is simplistic to conclude that because Luther did not form missionary societies, he did not support the mission of the gospel.[7] It is more accurate to point out that Luther's "field" for missionary work was limited to Christendom. Indeed, his reform of the church centered on the proclamation of the pure gospel of Jesus Christ in that "mission field" because, as Reformation historian Scott H. Hendrix notes, "the Reformers saw themselves in a missionary situation in which the faith had to be taught to a populace they judged to be inadequately informed."[8] As James A. Scherer writes,

> Since the Gospel had fallen into oblivion in Christendom—Luther's Gentiles being those who had never heard the pure Word of God preached in Germany—missionary obedience could only mean preaching the gospel anew. And since the distortion of the Gospel message had led to the degeneration of mission into ecclesiastical propaganda, forced conversions, crusades, and non-evangelical methods, Luther's obedience to the mission command meant re-establishing the church on its one true foundation of Jesus Christ and the Gospel.[9]

While the record of seventeenth-century Lutheran theologians regarding this question is mixed, the emergence of pietism in Germany and northern Europe spurred Lutherans to form and support missionary efforts.[10] The deep interest in missionary outreach by the pietists, "which had been largely left out of account by the representative of the major communions during the seventeenth century," compelled them to share the gospel to the whole world.[11] The Lutheran pietists were more willing to work outside of official church structures to spread the gospel to all people. By the

---

6. Öberg, *Luther and World Mission*, 5.
7. See Van Neste, "The Mangled Narrative," 3–13.
8. Hendrix, *Recultivating the Vineyard*, 172.
9. Scherer, "Luther and Mission," 1–8; Bunkowske, "Was Luther a Missionary?" 9–24; Elert, "Luther and 'Mission,'" 25–42.
10. Kolb, "'So Much Began in Halle,'" 26–35.
11. Stoeffler, *The Rise of Evangelical Pietism*, 19.

eighteenth century, Lutheran missionaries were sent to various countries, both to spread Christianity (as in the case of Lutheran missions to India, Indonesia, Tanzania, and other lands) and provide pastoral ministry to Lutheran immigrant communities elsewhere (as in the case of the American colonies).

Halle University in Germany was one center of mission activity. August Hermann Francke expanded the activities of the Halle Foundations (which included, among other things, founding orphanages) beyond the borders of German lands to include the German diaspora in eastern Europe and the American colonies, and to parts of the world with little or no exposure to the Christian gospel.[12] In 1706, the first Lutheran (and, in fact, the first Protestant) missionaries to India, Bartholomäus Zeigenbalg and Heinrich Plütschau, had received their training at Halle. Ziegenbalg both evangelized the Tamil people with the gospel and advocated for social justice. Tamil scholar Daniel Jeyaraj awarded Zeigenbalg the title, "The father of modern Protestant mission," pointing out that the much better-known British Baptist missionary William Carey—who remains the towering figure in most mission history narratives—would not arrive in India for another hundred years.[13]

Later, in 1742, Henry Melchior Muhlenberg was sent by Halle University to the American colonies. Muhlenberg's missionary enterprise to the colonies was less to evangelize non-believers than to "plant the church" among the German Lutheran immigrants who preceded him and who were so were hungry and thirsty for the gospel that they became easy targets for clergy "pretenders."[14] He described his mission strategy in his second journal entry: "Had myself transported to a city in a boat, looked for German people, and found several who said that they had no lack of physical nourishment but that they were gravely in need of spiritual

---

12. Kolb and Shantz, *An Introduction to German Pietism*, 126–43.
13. Wilson, "The Missionary India Never Forgot," n.p. See also Jeyaraj, "The First Lutheran Missionary Bartholomäus Ziegenbalg," 379–400.
14. Muhlenberg's journals offer reflections on the opportunity and challenge of evangelizing Native Americans, but his own focus was on serving those German Lutherans who were already believers. See for example, Tappert and Doberstein, eds., *The Notebook of a Colonial Clergyman*, 24–26. For examples of Muhlenberg's dealings with clergy "pretenders," see pp. 8–13.

nourishment, namely the Word of God and the holy sacraments in their language."[15] His missionary task was to preach God's Word to them, offer them the sacraments, provide pastoral care, connect congregations, and train other pastors to serve the needs of the German immigrants. Mission in Muhlenberg's context primarily meant serving those who were already baptized believers.

Lutherans historically have stressed their "evangelical" identity, meaning centered on the gospel—the "pure" gospel of justification by grace through faith—which is to be proclaimed to all people. While Lutheran theology has a missionary impulse, Lutheran ecclesiology has not always followed. Lutherans in North America, as in Europe, think of the church primarily as those gathered by the Holy Spirit through word and sacrament to receive and be comforted by the good news, and less as those who are sent out by the Holy Spirit to share their testimony of the good news with others. Craig Van Gelder and others have argued that defining the church by the Word and Sacraments in this way does not offer obvious resources for the church's sending.[16]

North American Lutherans live in a context today that is quite different from that of Muhlenberg's. In the 1990s, the Gospel and our Culture Network (GOCN) was founded by a group of primarily Reformed theologians inspired by Lesslie Newbigin's challenge that North America think of itself as a "mission field."[17] The GOCN began to study the context and culture of North America as the first step for doing mission.[18] Instead of asking, "How might we take the gospel into another culture?" as did traditional missionaries, they asked the question: What does it mean to be a missional church in "our" *North American* culture? What would it mean to be a missionary to one's own cultural context, a context that is increasingly post-Christian and pluralistic, and increasingly desperate for hope and reconciliation? Furthermore, it is a context

---

15. Tappert and Doberstein, *The Notebook of a Colonial Clergyman*, 1.
16. See, for example, Van Gelder, *The Essence of the Church*.
17. For more on the GOCN, see: https://gocn.org/
18. While they use the singular "culture," a study of "cultures" is more apt, since there are contextual differences not only between the US and Canada, but also between the many sub-cultures within each of these larger contexts.

in which the church has ceased to be a place of meaning and connection for those seeking the spiritual. The fastest growing religious affiliation in the United States today are the "Nones," those who have no religious affiliation. The 2017 report on the findings of PRRI's American Values Atlas states that "The religiously unaffiliated—those who identify as 'atheist,' 'agnostic,' or 'nothing in particular'—now account for nearly one-quarter (24%) of Americans. Since the early 1990s, this group has roughly tripled in size."[19] While very few of the Nones refer to themselves as "religious," many embrace the descriptor "spiritual but not religious," indicating their unease with religious practices and institutions on the one hand, and their interest in exploring the question of something "more" or transcendent, on the other hand. Diana Butler Bass's recent work suggests that there are those interested in exploring spirituality as a means to relationship with God and for making a difference in the world, in the lives of others, but have not found the church a conducive place for this exploration.[20] What does the mission of the church look like in such a context?

The Missio Dei *and* Missio Ecclesia

In order to answer this question, it is important first to consider an important distinction that reflects a shift in missiological thinking in the mid-twentieth century, between the *missio ecclesia* (the mission of the church) and the *missio Dei* (the mission of God). The term *mission* itself is rooted in classical trinitarian theology and historically was used exclusively in reference to the "missions" ("sendings") of the Son and the Spirit within the Godhead until the end of the sixteenth century.[21] This trinitarian foundation is important to emphasize, especially because the theological connection of mission to the Trinity was lost for much of the modern missionary movement. In the eighteenth and nineteenth centuries, mission was understood primarily in terms of the church; while mission was done for the sake of God's kingdom, it was viewed primarily an activity of the church itself. The church sent

---

19. Cox and Jones, "America's Changing Religious Identity," n.p.
20. Bass, *Christianity after Religion*, 20–26.
21. Bosch, *Transforming Mission*, 1.

missionaries into the world to spread the gospel, and care for those in need.

In the emerging ecclesiology, mission is not primarily an activity or even a purpose of the church. It is something God is doing into which the church is invited to participate. In this way, mission becomes central to the church's identity and nature because the church has been called into being by a "missional" God. As the great South African missiologist David Bosch once put it: "The classical doctrine of the *missio Dei* as God the Father sending the Son, and God the Father and the Son sending the Spirit [is] expanded to include yet another 'movement': Father, Son, and Holy Spirit sending the church into the world."[22] This makes mission "the result of God's initiative, rooted in God's purposes to restore and heal creation. 'Mission' means 'sending' and it is the central biblical theme describing the purpose of God's action in human history."[23] The church's being reflects that of the God who sends: the church is "essentially missionary," as Bosch states. "Here the church is not the sender but the one sent."[24] As the catchphrase, perhaps apocryphally, attributed to Rowan Williams stipulates, "It is not that the church has a mission. God's mission has a church."

This shift is often attributed to Karl Barth, who wrote in 1932 that the church's mission must be in response to the mission of God.[25] Twenty years later at the Willingen Conference on the International Missionary Council, Karl Hartenstein coined the phrase *missio Dei* in reference to the purposes and activities of God in and for the whole world, and not only the evangelization of the unreached nations. He wrote, "Mission is not just the conversion of the individual, nor just obedience to the word of the Lord, nor just the obligation to gather the church. It is the taking part in the sending of the Son, the *missio Dei,* with the holistic aim of establishing Christ's rule over all redeemed creation."[26]

---

22. Bosch, *Transforming Mission*, 390.
23. Guder, ed., *Missional Church*, 4.
24. Bosch, *Transforming Mission*, 372.
25. Bosch, *Transforming Mission*, 389–93; see also Van Gelder and Zscheile, *Missional Church in Perspective*, 15–40.
26. Cited by Engelsviken, "*Missio Dei*," 482n6.

The Willingen Conference also put a fresh emphasis on the trinitarian foundation of mission: "The missionary movement of which we are part has its source in the triune God Himself. Out of the depths of His love for us, the Father has sent forth His beloved Son to reconcile all things to Himself, that we and all [men] might, through the Spirit, be made one in Him with the Father, in that perfect love which is the very nature of God."[27] In making God rather than the church the reference point for mission, the Willingen conference affirmed the Christocentric center and the primacy of the church's agency for God's mission in the world.[28]

Since then, these shifts in understanding have continued to reshape missiology and the theology of mission. Both the World Council of Churches (WCC) and the Lutheran World Federation (LWF) have embraced the trinitarian foundation for mission and have connected the church's mission explicitly to the *missio Dei*. While proclamation and evangelism still have central roles in the church's mission, more holistic understandings of mission have emerged. For example, a 1988 LWF document defines mission as:

> Proclamation of the gospel, calling people to believe in Jesus Christ and to become members of the new community in Christ, participation in the work of peace and justice and in the struggle against all enslaving and dehumanizing powers are therefore an integral part of the mission of the church. All such activities point to the reality of the Reign of God and to its final realization at the fulfilment of history.[29]

Does God's Mission have a Scripture?

In light of the preceding, I now come to the question at the heart of this essay: If mission is central to God's being and identity, and if God's mission has a church, "Does God's mission also have a Scripture?" More specifically: What passage or passages in the Bible best help ground a theology of mission? Taking cues from the Reformation and the emerging theology of mission, any proposed scriptural texts must reflect God as the primary agent for mission, which is accomplished through the church. The

---

27. Engelsviken, "*Missio Dei*," 482.
28. Engelsviken, "*Missio Dei*," 486.
29. Lutheran World Federation, *Together in God's Mission*, 9.

remainder of this essay will consider and evaluate some scriptural passages as a basis for a theology of mission in light of these shifts, and the current context for mission in North America.

When one thinks about scriptural bases for mission, the first text that comes to mind is Matt 28:18–20, commonly known as "The Great Commission."[30] As David Bosch writes, "To many Protestants and more importantly to Evangelicals, the centrality or the Great Commission appears to be self-evident. It is even at times cited at the sole scriptural foundation for mission."[31] In spite of the fact that it was not until the late seventeenth century that it became a primary text for the church's mission and its use has been primarily in Anglo-Saxon circles, Matt 28:18–20 remains the "Magna Carta" of mission for most Protestants. This is true not only for overseas mission, but also for the domestic church growth movement, as Bosch notes. For example, in the case of church growth consultant, Donald McGavran, the "Great Commission" provides not only the major biblical foundation for mission, but also significant guidelines and methods for missionary work.

I would have numbered myself among these until about 16 years ago. I was attending a missiology conference in Aarhus, Denmark, at which Phillip Baker called for a 10-year moratorium on the use of Matt 28:16–20 as the foundational text for mission. He also issued a call to missiologists, church leaders, and other concerned Christians to explore other biblical passages as foundational mission texts.[32] He offered several reasons for his

---

30. The other leading contender is Acts 1:8, "You shall be my witnesses . . . to the ends of the earth," which is a particular favorite among Pentecostal Christians, in part because it is followed by the promise of "power from on high," that is the Holy Spirit, for this task. The language in Acts echoes that in the Lukan commission text. While there are passages in the Old Testament that have missional connotations, such as Isa 42:6–7, the witness of Israel lies its distinctive identity and practices. As David Bosch (*Transforming Mission*, 19) points out, "Israel would, however, not actually go out to the nations. Neither would Israel expressly call the nations to faith in Yahweh. So if there is 'missionary' in the Old Testament, it is God himself who will, as his eschatological deed par excellence, bring the nations to Jerusalem to worship him there together with his covenant people." See also Kaiser, *Mission in the Old Testament*.
31. Bosch, "Scope of Mission," 18.
32. Baker, "Mission and the New Creation," 39–52.

proposed moratorium. First, there is no internal evidence in Matthew's Gospel to warrant calling this the "great" commission. That is a later editorial addition that implies a value judgment not supported by the Gospel itself. Second, as noted above, this biblical text is "a late comer to the missiological scene."[33] Third, and perhaps most importantly, is the way that this text has been misused or interpreted out of context. Most Christians understand this text as referring to the "sending out" of disciples into the world to bring people to faith in Christ and into the churches. However, much of contemporary New Testament exegesis does not support this interpretation. By reading this passage in the context of the whole Gospel of Matthew, some New Testament scholars have argued that it has as much or more to do with people "inside the new community," as outside, or as Baker puts it, "the internal integrity of the church." He cites New Testament scholar David Smith, who argues that the purpose of Matt 28:16–20 is to create a community of disciples to live out its corporate life together with integrity.[34]

A fourth reason not explored by Baker is the exegetical matter of the opening words of the so-called Great Commission, "Go ye therefore." These words have acquired particular importance in Western missionary thinking, with the stress that many eighteenth and nineteenth century missiologists have put on the imperative, "go." However, many biblical scholars have pointed out that the Greek verb "to go" is often used as an auxiliary in Matthew's Gospel (as an aorist participle), "reinforcing the action of the main verb." As New Testament scholar Peter O'Brien states, "In emphasizing the main verb, no idea of going need be present at all. The core of the command is the making of disciples, not the going. The idea of sending, being sent (i.e. from one place to another) is secondary and un-emphasized, and as a result some have suggested the word 'go' is better left untranslated."[35]

For the purposes of this essay, the most obvious concern with using this text is that whether interpreted in terms of the church's call to discipleship or to being sent, Matt 28:16–20 focuses on what *the church* is called to do, and not on what God has done and

---

33. Baker, "Mission and the New Creation," 41.
34. Baker, "Mission and the New Creation," 42.
35. O'Brien, "The Great Commission of Matthew 28:18–20," 73.

is doing. The *missio Dei* is only implied in this text; the "Great Commission" does not articulate what God has accomplished through the incarnation, life, death, and resurrection of Jesus Christ and what difference that makes for the world.

The text that Phillip Baker proposed in its place does exactly that, however. He proposed as an alternative scriptural foundation for mission 2 Cor 5:14–21:

> So if anyone is in Christ, there is a new creation: everything old has passed away; see, everything has become new! All of this is from God, who reconciled us to himself through Christ, and has given us the ministry of reconciliation; that is, in Christ God was reconciling the world to himself, not counting their trespasses against them, and entrusting the message of reconciliation to us. So we are ambassadors for Christ, since God is making his appeal through us. We entreat you on behalf of Christ, be reconciled to God.

What is striking about this passage, as Baker himself points out, is that God is the primary agent in the "drama of the new creation."[36] God is the one reconciling the world to God's own self through Christ. Even in the act of proclamation, God is the primary actor. Note Paul's language here: God makes an appeal "through us." This scriptural passage teaches that God's mission is one of new creation, and God accomplishes that through reconciliation in Christ. The church's calling is to be ambassadors for Christ, to point to the reconciliation that God makes possible through Christ's death and resurrection.

Robert Schreiter posits that the context of the world today calls for "special attention to the praxis of reconciliation as a newly emerging paradigm of mission."[37] Reconciliation happens at the vertical (between God and human beings) as well as horizontal (between individual human beings and human groups) and cosmic (the whole creation) levels; the horizontal and cosmic dimensions are made possible by the vertical. Lutheran Raphael Malpica-Padilla likewise states, "God's mission to the world is that of

---

36. Baker, "Mission and the New Creation," 43.
37. Malpica-Padilla, "Accompaniment as an Alternative Model," 92. See also Schreiter, "Reconciliation as a New Paradigm of Mission," n.p.; see also Schreiter, *Reconciliation*.

restoring community, and *reconciliation* becomes a prominent theological dimension of that mission."[38] This passage from 2 Cor 5 serves especially well as a biblical foundation for understanding the *missio Dei* for churches rooted in the Reformation, as it resonates with the Reformers' focus on God's reconciling action in Jesus Christ for us, and through us. Mission begins with what God has done for us and what God is doing through us, not on what we as the church do for God.

Following Baker, if one takes this text as the foundation for the *missio Dei*, then one can ask: What might the *church's mission* look like in light of this text? For Schreiter, reconciliation is the process for engaging mission as well as the goal of mission. The church is called to participate in God's reconciling work through a ministry of reconciliation. Schreiter's biblical understanding of reconciliation is outlined in five points. First, God, not the church, is the author of reconciliation; we participate in God's work as God's ambassadors. Second, the healing of victims is God's first concern in the process of reconciliation. Third, reconciliation encompasses healing for both victim and wrongdoer. The process of healing begins with truth-telling, uncovering what Schreiter calls "the narratives of the lie," and the seeking of justice, which then can lead to the rebuilding of relationships. Fourth, for Christians, the way to address suffering is by placing it in Christ's suffering, death, and resurrection. In this way, Christians can escape its destructive power and have their hope sustained. Finally, reconciliation will only be complete when all things are fulfilled eschatologically in Jesus Christ (Eph 1:10); until that day, we only experience it in part, even as we life in hope of its fullness.[39] Building off of Schreiter's framework, Malpica-Padilla breaks down the church's ministry of reconciliation into three steps: repentance, restoration, and recreation.[40] Canadian ethicist Marilyn Legge agrees, stating that "negotiating mission for the 21st century starts by giving attention to the massive suffering that exists, as well as the yearning for healing, justice, and mutual relationship," which in the Canadian context suggests attention to the historical

---

38. Malpica-Padilla, "Accompaniment as an Alternative Model," 91.
39. Schreiter, "Reconciliation as a New Paradigm for Mission," 2–3.
40. Malpica-Padilla, "Accompaniment as an Alternative Model," 94–96.

legacy of the churches' mission with Aboriginal peoples through residential schools.[41]

The Church's Commission in Light of God's Mission

With this framework in mind, we can return to Matt 28:16–20—and the other "commissioning" texts in the Gospels—in order to unpack the mission of the church in light of this interpretation of the *missio Dei*.[42] The "commission" in Matthew 28 is not "go," but "make disciples." Being a disciple in Matthew's Gospel means living out the teaching of Jesus, and includes a life of love and justice. For Matthew this involves "making new believers sensitive to the needs of others, opening their eyes and hearts to recognize injustice, suffering, oppression and the plight of those who have fallen by the wayside."[43]

On the other hand, one can find an explicit commission to "Go to the world" in Mark 16:14–18, but Mark's commission has been overshadowed by Matthew's more famous version. There are likely two reasons for this. First, biblical scholars largely agree that this is not the original ending of Mark's Gospel, but was added by a later editor to bring the conclusion of Mark's Gospel more into line with the other Gospels. Second, it not only refers to signs and wonders with which most ecumenical Protestants are uncomfortable (i.e., healing, speaking in tongues, exorcisms), it also refers to signs and wonders with which most Pentecostals—apart from a very small sect of Appalachian holiness Christians— also are uncomfortable (i.e., the practice of snake-handling and poison drinking).

It is important to point out that the only thing Jesus commands his disciples in this Markan text is to go and proclaim the good news to creation. The rest are either promises (the one who

---

41. Legge, "Negotiating Mission," 121. See also the essays in Vol. 31, issue 1 of *Consensus: A Canadian Journal of Public Theology* (2016), "Journeying Together Toward Truth and Reconciliation."

42. As noted above, while Acts 1:8 is also a commissioning text, it will not be treated separately in this article due to the focus on the Gospels.

43. Bosch, *Transforming Mission*, 81.

believes and is baptized with be saved) or signs that accompany those who proclaim the gospel. Pentecostal and charismatic Christians often highlight "signs and wonders," such as healing and other forms of deliverance, for manifesting the power of God. As signs, they always point to Jesus, to the in-breaking kingdom of God inaugurated in his life, death, and resurrection, which his disciples are to preach to the whole creation.

The last sign is introduced with the conditional conjunctive "if"—if the disciples drink anything deadly, it will not hurt them. Since there are no New Testament accounts of the disciples drinking poison or handling snakes, some scholars wonder whether the "if" may in fact apply to both. Either way, Jesus does not command his followers to do such things. They are included rather as examples of signs that may accompany the proclaiming of the gospel, examples of God's providence if harm or danger comes to someone who is sharing the good news of Jesus, whether by accident (e.g., Acts 28:1–6)[44] or intentionally.[45]

Although it is more commonly associated with Pentecostalism for the reasons just noted, Mark 16:16–18 is the New Testament "commissioning text" most frequently preached on by Martin Luther (much more than Matt 28)! The reason is found in v. 15: Jesus' command to "go into all the world and proclaim the good news to all creation," which Mark defines at the outset of his Gospel as the coming of the kingdom in Jesus Christ. This, of course, is at the heart of Luther's Reformation. The church's specific calling is nothing other than proclaiming God's reconciling love to the whole of creation. The church proclaims the good news through word and deed, so that all may know the promise of God's

---

44. The one narrative account in the New Testament of a snakebite is one that occurs by accident, not as something sought after. A viper attacked Paul in Malta while he was tending a fire, but he shook it off and was not harmed (Acts 28:1–6).

45. For example, Ludwig Nommensen, a nineteenth-century German missionary to Sumatra (Indonesia) unwittingly consumed poison put in his food by the Batak people on at least three occasions, yet he remained unharmed. This not only baffled the Batak people, but also prompted one of his would-be killers to listen to his sermons, which then led him to be baptized. Nommensen came to be known as the Apostle to the Batak. Lehmann, *A Biographical Study of Ingwer Ludwig Nommensen (1834–1918)*, 136–38.

great love for them in Jesus and the benefits that entails, specifically: life, salvation, and the forgiveness of sins.

The elements of discipleship and the proclamation of the gospel to all of creation, as found in the Matthean and Markan commissioning texts, are important aspects of the church's mission to be ambassadors of reconciliation, the *missio Dei*. However, the Lukan and Johannine commissioning texts, which will be explored below, are particularly helpful in unpacking the church's mission as rooted in 2 Cor 5, for two reasons. First, these texts offer more specific content to the "good news" which is to be proclaimed and given witness, that is, repentance and forgiveness of sins, which are key elements of God's reconciling work. Second, each clearly focuses on the cross and resurrection of Jesus as the foundation of the church's mission (whether explicitly, as in Luke, or implicitly as in John, as Jesus shows the disciples his wounded hands) and on the accompanying and empowering role of the Holy Spirit for their mission.

In Luke 24, Jesus' words commissioning the disciples come after the narrative of Jesus joining the two unnamed disciples on the road to Emmaus. Jesus states plainly that they "are witnesses of these things" (Luke 14:48), a commission that is echoed and strengthened in Acts 1:8 ("You will be my witnesses in Jerusalem, in all Judea and Samaria, and to the ends of the earth"). In the 2004 Lutheran World Federation document "Mission in Context," it is the Emmaus Road encounter—not the "commission" that follows it—that was highlighted as the basis for the church's mission. As the document states, the Emmaus model "speaks for and enlightens a hermeneutical spiral approach to mission, an approach that is reflective of the interaction between contexts, theology, and practice. It is also considered to be the best model, at this time, to convey the understanding of mission as accompaniment."[46] The document further elucidates,

> The mission encounter begins as Jesus walks with the disciples on the Emmaus road, sharing in their pain by listening to them as they tell their story (verse 18). Jesus then interprets the scriptures and shares with the disciples a theological understanding of God's saving act in

---

46. Lutheran World Federation, *Mission in Context*, 7–8.

history and reveals to them in the breaking of the bread the presence of the resurrected one in their midst. With their eyes opened to the in-breaking reign of God, the disciples, transformed by the encounter and celebrating Christ's reconciling presence, go out, empowered to share this good news with their nurturing community and others.[47]

Accompaniment also has emerged as the central hermeneutical key and methodological tool for engaging mission for the Evangelical Lutheran Church in America (ELCA). As Raphael Malpica-Padilla explains, "Accompaniment is walking together in solidarity which is characterized by mutuality and interdependence. The basis for this accompaniment, what the New Testament calls *koinonia*, is found in the God-human relationship in which God accompanies us in Jesus Christ through the power of the Holy Spirit."[48] After the encounter on the road to Emmaus in Luke 24, Jesus appears to his disciples and opens their minds to understand the Scriptures. Then, in more of a promise than a commission, he tells them that they shall be his witnesses (to show people Jesus!), and then promises to clothe them with power from on high, the Holy Spirit, to enable them to do this.

In John 20:19–23, the commission is more explicit ("As the Father sends me, so I send you"), and as Jesus breathes on them the Holy Spirit, and gives them the authority to forgive sins. Here we have in both Luke and John an intimate linking together of pneumatology and mission, which read in the larger context of John's Gospel, particularly chs. 14–16, offers additional resources for thinking about the church's mission as accompaniment. Drawing on John's Gospel, the Holy Spirit becomes the primary "accompanier" for the church (and the world)—the *paraclete,* literally the one who "walks alongside of one," or, the one who accompanies. As the *paraclete,* the Spirit not only enters into solidarity with us but abides in us (John 14:17). In the Johannine account, the Spirit's accompanying and abiding also brings conviction and truth-telling (16:8, 16:13), teaching and guidance (14:26, 16:13), testifying (15:26–27), and ultimately, the gift of forgiveness and reconciliation (20:22–23).

---

47. Lutheran World Federation, *Mission in Context*, 8.
48. Malpica-Padilla, "Accompaniment as an Alternative Model," 88.

Conclusion

The story of the decline of the "mainline" churches (which, as some have suggested, have become "sideline") is all too well known these days. Even evangelical denominations are starting to see worship attendance and participation decrease. These shifts are causing many congregations in North America to wrestle with what their "mission" ought to be in the world. Elsewhere, I have written that the wrong question is "what do we do?" and the better, more faithful question for the church is, "Who is God calling us to be?"[49] The church is called to be a missional people because we believe in a missional God, who chose us to be sent into the world through the incarnation of the Son and the outpouring of the Spirit.

In this essay, I have suggested that it is important to frame our understanding of the church's mission by first considering what God's mission is in the world—a mission of reconciliation. The church is called to participate in this mission in an increasingly polarized context that includes an increasing number of people who, while they reject institutional religion, may be open to the reconciling, transforming message of the gospel. A foundational Scripture for understanding God's mission is the world is 2 Cor 5:14–21. The "commissioning texts" in the four Gospels can further guide the churches in their mission to be "ambassadors of reconciliation," through ministries of discipleship, proclamation, witness, and accompaniment.

Bibliography

Baker, Phillip. "Mission and the New Creation." In *The Role of Mission in Lutheran Theology*, edited by Viggo Mortensen, 39–52. Århus: Centre for Multireligious Studies, University of Århus, 2003.

Bass, Diana Butler. *Christianity after Religion: The End of the Church and the Birth of a New Spiritual Awakening.* New York: HarperOne, 2012.

---

49. See Peterson, *Who is the Church?*

Bosch, David J. "Scope of Mission." *International Review of Mission* 7.289 (1984) 17–32.

———. *Transforming Mission: Paradigm Shifts in Theology of Mission*. American Society of Missiology Series 16. Maryknoll, NY: Orbis, 1991.

Bunkowske, Eugene W. "Was Luther a Missionary?" In *The Lutherans in Mission: Essays in Honor of Won Yong Ji*, edited by Alan D. Scott, 9–24. Lutheran Society for Missiology Book Series. Fort Wayne, IN: Lutheran Society for Missiology, 2000.

Cox, Daniel, and Robert P. Jones. "America's Changing Religious Identity." *Public Religion Research Institute (PRRI)*, 6 September 2017. Online: https://www.prri.org/research/american-religious-landscape-christian-religiously-unaffiliated/.

Elert, Werner. "Luther and 'Mission.'" In *The Lutherans in Mission: Essays in Honor of Won Yong Ji*, edited by Alan D. Scott, 25–42. Lutheran Society for Missiology Book Series. Fort Wayne, IN: Lutheran Society for Missiology, 2000.

Engelsviken, Tormod. "*Missio Dei*: The Understanding and Misunderstanding of a Theological Concept in European Churches and Missiology." *International Review of Mission* 92.367 (2003) 481–97.

Guder, Darrell, ed. *Missional Church: A Vision for the Sending of the Church in North America*. The Gospel and Our Culture Network Series. Grand Rapids: Eerdmans, 1998.

Hendrix, Scott H. *Recultivating the Vineyard: The Reformation Agendas of Christianization*. Louisville: Westminster/John Knox, 2004.

Jeyaraj, Daniel. "The First Lutheran Missionary Bartholomäus Ziegenbalg: His Concepts of Culture and Mission from a Postcolonial Perspective." *Swedish Missiological Themes* 93.2 (2005) 379–400.

Kaiser, Walter C., Jr. *Mission in the Old Testament: Israel as a Light to the Nations*. Grand Rapids: Baker, 2000.

Kolb, Robert. "Foreword." In *Luther and World Mission: A Historical and Systematic Study*, by Ingemar Öberg, vii. Translated by Dean Apel. St. Louis: Concordia Publishing House, 2007.

———. "'So Much Began in Halle': The Mission Program that Sent to Muhlenberg to America." *Concordia Historical Institute Quarterly* 84.3 (2011) 26–35.

Kolb, Robert, and Douglas Shantz. *An Introduction to German Pietism: Protestant Renewal at the Dawn of Modern Europe*. Baltimore: Johns Hopkins, 2013.

Legge, Marilyn J. "Negotiating Mission: A Canadian Stance." *International Review of Mission* 93.368 (2004) 119–30.

Lehmann, Martin E. *A Biographical Study of Ingwer Ludwig Nommensen (1834–1918), Pioneer Missionary to the Bataks of Sumatra*. Lewiston, NY: Edwin Mellen, 1996.

Lutheran World Federation. *Mission in Context: Transformation, Reconciliation, Empowerment. An LWF Contribution to the Understanding and Practice of Mission*. Geneva: Lutheran World Federation, 2004.

———. *Together in God's Mission: An LWF Contribution to the Understanding of Mission*. Geneva: LWF, 1988.

Malpica-Padilla, Raphael. "Accompaniment as an Alternative Model for the Practice of Mission." *Trinity Seminary Review* 29.1 (2008) 87–98.

O'Brien, Peter. "The Great Commission of Matthew 28:18–20: A Missionary Mandate, or Not?" *Reformed Theological Review* 35.3 (1978) 61–69.

Öberg, Ingemar. *Luther and World Mission: A Historical and Systematic Study*. Translated by Dean Apel. St. Louis, Concordia Publishing House, 2007.

Peterson, Cheryl M. *Who is the Church? An Ecclesiology for the Twenty-First Century*. Minneapolis: Fortress, 2013.

Scherer, James A. "Luther and Mission: A Rich but Untested Potential." In *The Lutherans in Mission: Essays in Honor of Won Yong Ji*, edited by Alan D. Scott, 1–8. Lutheran Society for Missiology Book Series. Fort Wayne, IN: Lutheran Society for Missiology, 2000.

Schreiter, Robert J. *Reconciliation: Mission and Ministry in a Changing Social Order*. Maryknoll, NY: Orbis, 1992.

———. "Reconciliation as a New Paradigm of Mission." Conference on World Mission and Evangelism, Come Holy Spirit—Heal and Reconcile (Called in Christ to be Reconciling and Healing Communities), Athens, Greece, 14 May 2005. Online: http://www.sedosmission.org/web/en/mission-articles-2/doc_view/560-reconciliation-as-a-new-paradigm-of-mission.

Stoeffler, F. Ernest. *The Rise of Evangelical Pietism*. Leiden: Brill, 1970.

Tappert, Theodore G., and John W. Doberstein, eds. *The Notebook of a Colonial Clergyman*. Minneapolis: Fortress, 1998.

Van Gelder, Craig. *The Essence of the Church: A Community Created by the Spirit*. Grand Rapids: Baker, 2000.

Van Gelder, Craig, and Dwight J. Zscheile. *Missional Church in Perspective: Mapping Trends and Shaping the Conversation*. Grand Rapids: Baker Academic, 2011.

Van Neste, Ray. "The Mangled Narrative of Missions and Evangelism in the Reformation." *Southeastern Theological Review* (2017) 1–7.

Wilson, Sarah Hinlicky. "The Missionary India Never Forgot." *Christianity Today*, 2 October 2017. Online: http://www.christianitytoday.com/ct/2014/october-web-only/missionary-india-never-forgot-bartholomaeus-ziegenbalg.html.

From the Will to Power to the Power of Weakness:
Toward a Post-Christendom Evangelism

Rick Richardson
Wheaton College, Wheaton, IL, USA

Introduction

In this article, I engage with the late modern or postmodern critique of metanarratives or Grand Stories. The Christian gospel is one such Grand Story that has been subjected to thoroughgoing critique in our day. In a post-Christendom culture, many have dismissed the Christian Grand Story without even hearing it. It is dismissed merely on the basis of the culture-wide conviction that there is no Grand Story that is true for everybody, and that people who believe that they have a Grand Story that is true for everybody are misguided at best and manipulative, judgmental, intolerant, and oppressive at worst.

I want to take a fresh look at the postmodern critique of all metanarratives,[1] with the goal of gaining insight into the basis of the critique and with the hope of gaining insight into how better to communicate the Christian Grand Story in our post-Christendom culture. It is my conviction that many evangelicals have not really understood the critique and its basis, and therefore have not responded to it substantively. As a Christian professor and an apologist for years on secular campuses, I am committed to hearing

---

1. I use the term "postmodern" in this paper in the way that Francois Lyotard used it in his book *The Postmodern Condition*. I could also use "late modern" or "hypermodern" as terms describing the natural result of the breakdown of the modernist project that was based on the confidence and dependency on rationality as an effective means to gain universal truth, on complete objectivity as a real and attainable goal in human pursuits, on hyper-individualism that disregards cultural and social influences in the production of truth, and on evolutionary progress as the defining principle of Western history.

deeply the critique of seekers and skeptics in our post-Christendom culture, and responding in hopefully comprehensible and compelling ways to that critique. My goal is not to adopt a postmodern worldview but rather to speak plausibly and even persuasively into it.

At the heart of this paper is the goal of recovering a more biblically-rooted vision of evangelism, of communicating the good news. Paul the apostle communicated the gospel and planted the church in a pre-Christendom world, and he understood that the fundamental dynamic of an evangelism that could gain purchase and bear fruit was captured in the words of the Holy Spirit to him in the midst of profound feelings of vulnerability, weakness, and suffering, "My grace is sufficient for you, for my power is made perfect in weakness" (2 Cor 12:9).[2] This convergence of our weakness with God's power is at the heart of a decolonized and decolonizing post-Christendom evangelism, pursued out of weakness and vulnerability rather than from a position of social power. Paul's litany of his own suffering and weakness in advancing the gospel, as listed in 2 Cor 4:7–12, is what might be called the Pauline model of apostolic witness: Treasures of God's power and authority wrapped up and shining through in profound human vulnerability, weakness, suffering, persecution, and death. As Paul says in 1 Cor 2:3–4, "I came to you in weakness and in fear and in much trembling . . . with a demonstration of the Spirit and of power." I suggest that this model of profound human vulnerability, coupled with the genuine presence of Christ, is possibly the most important key to witness in post-Christendom contexts. The communication of the Christian metanarrative into post-Christendom contests must come with profound humility, vulnerability, suffering, and weakness, or else it will be received and interpreted as a power play, a dominance extending activity that lacks moral plausibility in our contemporary world.

---

2. All biblical quotes are from the New Revised Standard Version unless otherwise indicated.

Approach

My method in this article is to practice the discipline of enlarged thinking, or double vision in relation to the postmodern critique of metanarratives. In his book *Exclusion and Embrace*, Miroslav Volf challenges us to practice this "enlarged thinking" as we respond to our critics and even our adversaries. Our model is God, who, in the atonement, practiced self-giving love toward the enemy with the goal of embrace. God made room in God's very identity for God's enemy, hostile humanity. God made room for hostile humanity by becoming one of us, even identifying with us in our sinfulness.[3] God's goal was to take us into God's very being.

God is also our model in that God did not become less of who God is in this radical identification, but only more fully and deeply who God is as holy love. We, too, as we listen much more deeply to our critic and adversary, are not aiming to become our adversary, or lose our identity, but rather to fulfill and express our identity. In his unpacking of enlarged thinking, Volf was clearer about the embrace, the listening and being changed by our adversary. He was not always as clear and cogent about the sense in which exclusion still operates in any healthy identity, in which we maintain, deepen, and ultimately fulfill that identity. This tension between listening deeply and being changed by the incisive postmodern critique of Grand Stories and their potentially-destructive social impact on the one hand, and even more deeply embracing and boldly proclaiming our unique Christian Grand Story on the other hand is the tension this paper will make explicit.

Volf calls enlarged thinking "double vision." Double vision is making space in ourselves for the other, and then letting their perspectives correct ours, sometimes finding in their voices the silenced voices of our own tradition. If we make space for the other, even the enemy, as God made space, unlike God, we will find our own sinfulness and error in ways we never expected. The steps of double vision include:

    1. Step outside ourselves
    2. Enter their social world

---

3. See Matt 3:13–15; 2 Cor 5:21.

3. Take them into our inner world
4. Repeat the process[4]

You may notice that these steps do not adequately identify but seem only to assume the ways in which we hold onto what we bring into the encounter, including our traditions, stories, and sense of identity. My goal is to emphasize each side of the encounter when we experience the critique of others. We are changed in our very identity by that encounter. But we also hold on to what we have received and have already become. We practice embrace but not without solid boundaries based on our roots.

We are living in the same tension Paul lived in as an apostle sent to a radically new culture, Gentile culture. At times Paul emphasizes what we hold onto, as in Gal 1:8, when he says, "But even if we or an angel from heaven should preach a gospel other than the one we preached to you, let him be eternally condemned." At other times, Paul emphasizes how very fluid we need to be in order to embody the gospel in a different culture. "I have become all things to all people so that by all possible means I might save some." Often evangelical Christians have summed up this tension by saying that we are to hold onto the old, old message, the never changing gospel. But we are to communicate that message in ever changing and newly contextualized ways. As we shall see in the paper, this formulation of the tension is not adequate and often not even accurate given how culturally connected to Christendom contexts of social power and dominance that these formulations have often been.

So, what is the postmodern critique of metanarratives or Grand Stories? What can we learn from that critique? How does what we learn affect the message we communicate, the model of life we propose, and the methods through which our communication tales place? These questions provide a framework for the rest of the paper. First, this paper explores the postmodern critique of grand stories, owning up to ways that critique has been valid and sometimes incisively so about Christendom tendencies to communicate and propagate Christian faith for the purpose of extending a self-

---

4. Volf, *Exclusion and Embrace*, 252.

centered will to power. Second, I turn to a project of reclaiming the gold of the Christian grand narrative without the dross of a self-centered will to power at its heart. Finally, I suggest specific applications for how we might proceed in formulating and communicating the Christian metanarrative in a post-Christendom world in which God's power and our weakness, vulnerability, and suffering become intertwined.

The Postmodern Critique of Grand Stories

The Will to Power

I find much that is prophetic, helpful, and biblical in the postmodern critique of Grand Stories and the ways that those Grand Stories were developed and then functioned within history. At heart, as Volf reminds us, postmodernism is a program against exclusion.[5]

Friedrich Nietzsche and Ludwig Wittgenstein were probably the two most influential shapers of the foundations of the postmodern critique of Grand Stories. Nietzsche was the philosopher of power. The postmodern critique about truth and its function in supporting and legitimizing power is rooted in Nietzsche's reflection on the will to power. Nietzsche celebrated the will to power, finding it at the heart of all human reality. In his classic, *Thus Spoke Zarathustra*, Nietzsche proclaims through Zarathustra: "The will itself, the will to power, the unexhausted, procreative will of life is the good, the very heart of life."[6] Zarathustra goes on: "Hear then my word, and test whether I have crawled into the very heart of life and into the very roots of its heart. Where I found the living, there I found the will to power; and even in the will of those who serve, I found the will to be master."[7] Rather than despairing at human self-interest and the hidden will to power, Nietzsche exalts it. His hero is the Superman, or Overman (*Ubermensch*), who overcomes Man by creating his own reality and values according to his own taste and by his own strength of will. The poem "Invictus" by William Ernest Henley comes to mind:

---

5. Volf, *Exclusion and Embrace*, 63.
6. Nietzsche, *The Portable Nietzsche*, 226.
7. Nietzsche, *The Portable Nietzsche*, 226.

Out of the night that covers me,
Black as the pit from pole to pole,
I thank whatever gods may be
For my unconquerable soul . . .

I am the master of my fate,
I am the captain of my soul.[8]

(Though, differentiating the two, Henley's hero had bloodied but unbowed head, a picture of noble suffering, and Nietzsche's hero would more likely have had bloodied and overbearing hands.) Nietzsche despises the Christian faith and all Grand Stories that hide this will to power under the guise of virtue and democracy and equality and repression of the passions. To him, all such Grand Values are driven by the envy and jealousy of small men to bring all men down to their level: "Socrates and Plato are both symptoms of degeneration. Value judgments about life are never true, because those who judge are always an interested party, even a bone of contention."[9]

Nietzsche critiqued Christian faith for its repressive, leveling, hidden will to power by small men over great men.[10] But he also critiqued the Grand Stories of emancipation and democracy. In prescient ways, he saw the end result of the whole Enlightenment project of the rational and empirical search for truth. Underneath the search for truth is always the agenda of self-interest. No truth is not also an expression of this self-interest. The rational faculty incorporates this pervasive presence of self-interest, and so undermines its very foundational claims to objectivity and neutrality. There is no objective truth, and there is no way to get from "is" to "ought," from empirical observation to ethical values. In the search for truth was the inescapable and overwhelming expression

---

8. Henley, "Invictus."
9. Nietzsche, *The Portable Nietzsche*, 474.
10. I use the gendered noun "men" in this section because Nietzsche did.

of the will to power. In a fallen world, there is no truth that is not also distorted self-serving power.

Even logic itself is now suspect. Logic can equally well be used to reject slavery and other forms of injustice, or instead to support and legitimize slavery and other forms of injustice. Logic is thus often used in the expression of this self-serving will to power. Thus, Nietzsche paved the way for Francois Lyotard and Michel Foucault and others who saw this self-serving will to power as the driving force behind all Grand Stories. Francois Lyotard first defined postmodern: "Simplifying to the extreme, I define *postmodern* as incredulity toward metanarratives."[11] This incredulity first emerges out of being honest and analytical about the results in history of all Grand Stories at one point or another:

> In the West, we tell our story as a story of reason, enlightenment and civilization, contrasting it with the story of brutality and barbarity of backward and primitive cultures. But is the story true? It makes us feel superior and it justifies our colonial spirit. But in light of slavery, the Holocaust, and the extermination of Native races in America, how can we think it true? Our technology and bureaucracy have given us more sophisticated, large scale, and removed forms of brutality, but probably also far more effective forms of brutality. Savages do not have the potential for genocide as more modern societies do.[12]

You can also look at the Grand Story of Marxism that resulted in the authoritarian and even totalitarian bureaucracy of the Soviet Union. Or you can look at the Christian Grand Story, the story that supported the Crusades, or the Inquisition, or the Church's silence in Germany during the Holocaust, or the Church's history with slavery, or her attitudes toward women, or her contemporary battles with Muslims. The Christian Grand Story has been oppressive, as have all metanarratives to one degree or another, from the perspective of postmodern critics. And there is more than a grain of truth in their critique.

What Christians face from people in a post-Christendom culture when they claim that Jesus is the only way, is what all representatives of Grand, totalizing Stories face, when they seek to

---

11. Lyotard, *The Postmodern Condition*, xxiv.
12. Volf, *Exclusion and Embrace*, 59.

persuade other people that their way is the only right way. We face skepticism, distrust, and the conviction that behind this Grand Story lies the hidden agenda of the self-serving will to power. And that skepticism and distrust is not without basis. Even in the competitive, adversarial, and politicized ways we respond to the distrust of others, we can often demonstrate our own hidden drive for control, power, and dominance, and so reinforce the very distrust we had hoped to disarm. We Christians too often strive to synthesize the cross (truth) and the sword (coercive power) and the dollar (material power) in the service of self, at least ever since Constantine, whether we pursue that synthesis in our rhetoric, our economics, our racial theories, our military pursuits, or our religion.

Our Christian Grand Story has too often failed to separate the cross, the sword, and the dollar. Marva Dawn asks us a very haunting question about our "unchanging message." She explores the role of larger forces, heavenly and earthly, in their influence over even the shape and content of our "unchanging message": "How have the very powers themselves conspired to leave us with a gospel and ethic that perpetuates their control?"[13] In other words, what gets left out of our "unchanging message" so that the gospel no longer leads us to freedom from an unholy marriage between the cross and the sword and the dollar? Why has our Christian Grand Story so easily been used to support slavery, silence in the face of genocide, holy war against infidels, abusive relations of power between men and women, and between Caucasians and People of Color, and unjust economic relations? We must adequately grapple with how adaptable and useful Christians have made the Christian Grand Story to all kinds of injustice and to self-serving expressions of the Christian will to power. Otherwise, our plausibility, credibility, and even moral standing as advocates of a Grand Story that we believe to be true for everyone will be looked upon as oppressive, narrow, judgmental, and socially destructive. And not without good reason.

How does this self-serving will to power operate in our Grand Stories? Is a self-serving will to power inherent in every Grand Story, or is that self-serving will to power merely the way we

---

13. Dawn, *Powers, Weakness, and the Tabernacling of God*, 9.

misuse Grand Stories? As a committed Christian, I believe our Grand Story to be ultimately liberating and not oppressive. But I am also convinced that the human tendency toward the self-centered will to power, pleasure, and fame have distorted our knowledge and language about the good news of God. Michel Foucault addresses the ways these distortions can operate within a society or community by insightfully exploring the links between knowledge and power:

> In any society, there are manifold relations of power which permeate, characterize, and constitute the social body, and those relations of power cannot themselves be established, consolidated, and implemented without the production, accumulation, circulation, and functioning of a discourse. That discourse is that society's truth. I would say that we are forced to produce the truth of power that our society demands, of which it has need in order to function.[14]

A society produces the truth, or discourse, that it needs in order to function and reinforce its power relations. This reality helps illuminate how good church people in Bible-believing, Southern, predominately-white church, denominations could generate and then circulate "truths" about African American people as inferior and then stories from Sacred Writ like the story of the "curse of Ham" that legitimized enslaving "inferior people to civilize and reform them" in a destructive system of dehumanization and control for 150 years.[15]

A further implication is that when societies polarize around different versions of truth and knowledge, as is happening right now in American society, the production of knowledge and discourse in such a divided society will create nearly incommensurable mental and conversational worlds. Two or more versions of reality circulate using language and terms in two very contrasting ways, producing a culture war in which communication and understanding between the two worlds so created is nearly impossible. Often the driving force behind the creation of these alternate language worlds is a self-centered will to power. Christendom societies

---

14. Foucault, *Power/Knowledge*, 93.
15. See Emerson and Smith, *Divided by Faith*, 21–50; Tisby, *The Color of Compromise*.

have too often reflected these dynamics well. We have produced the "truth" that justified our maintenance and enforcement of our social and political power. This dynamic is one of the roots of both colonialism in the past and Christian nationalism up through today.

So first, postmodern critics have come to grips from an historical perspective with how pervasively Grand Stories have been used to achieve and legitimize dominance and injustice out of self-interest. But postmodern thinkers have taken their critique to an even more fundamental level. Postmodern thinkers have grappled with the nature of language itself. The conclusion? Self-serving bias does not just operate in the ways we use language, it operates in the ways we create language. Let us unpack how some thinkers have come to that conclusion.

The Will to Power in the Creation of Language

Jacques Derrida is certainly one of the most brilliant and influential advocates of the critique of the nature of language. Derrida shows how language itself is inherently unjust and self-serving. Then he proposes a method, called deconstruction, for overcoming the very exclusion and injustice that language itself fosters. As I have talked with evangelical Christians, I have found widespread misunderstanding and misconstrual of Derrida's basic program against exclusion. Derrida, like other postmodern thinkers, is battling for awareness about the self-serving will to power, and the ways that self-serving will to power is integrated into the very nature of language creation and usage.

Derrida suggests that all language systems have been built around polar or binary opposites.[16] God/devil, Christian/pagan, civilized/barbarian, good/evil, man/woman, Christian/Muslim, white/colored, rational/insane, rich/poor, proletariat/bourgeoisie, strong/weak and many other binary opposites lie at the heart of our most common Western Grand Stories and the languages used to express those stories. Those language terms have no meaning outside of the whole system of thinking and of worldview that lies

---

16. Derrida, *Writing and Difference*, 3–30.

behind those terms. And in each Grand Story, and in each corresponding system of language games, one term or group is preferred and the other is marginalized. The postmodern critique arises out of this experience of oppression and marginalization for the less valued term or group.

Some who analyze race issues have embraced these insights from Derrida. Kimberle Williams Crenshaw is one of those who has suggested that in the arena of race, similar dichotomies have come to dominate the discourse and the racial imagination of many Americans. She cites the following examples in which good values and characteristics have become associated with people of a white racial background and bad characteristics have become associated (in the discourse and the imagination) with Black people:[17]

Historical Oppositional Dualities

White Images	Black Images
Industrious	Lazy
Intelligent	Unintelligent
Moral	Immoral
Knowledgeable	Ignorant
Enabling Culture	Disabling culture
Law-abiding	Criminal
Responsible	Shiftless
Virtuous	Lascivious

Derrida wants to overcome the inherent injustice rooted in the nature of language itself. Derrida spares no one in his critique, whether Christian, Marxist, humanist, or postmodern.

Derrida's method is also worth considering. Derrida recognized that texts are full of tension. Language is often used in ways that reinforce the dominance of one term or group over other terms or groups. But Derrida also recognized that such simple readings of texts often ignore crucial tensions that actually undo some of the very dominance that the text is seemingly trying to promote.

---

17. Crenshaw, "Race, Reform, and Retrenchment," 103–25.

So Derrida de-centers the central term in a text, with the goal of setting language free from its dominance/suppression dynamics. At the same time, deconstruction carried to its logical conclusion erases meaning inherent in texts—which is not something biblical Christians committed to the authority of Scripture can embrace.

So, the goal of postmodern critique is to overcome and subvert relations of dominance that have been destructive. These relationships of dominance are subverted in different ways by different thinkers. But always the goal is subverting relations of power and dominance. At the heart of the effort is the commitment to let the "Other" speak, influence, and be central. In the end, it is not the reversal of power, but a new way to pursue discourse. We pursue discourse through the dialogue between opposites. The Other is now a valued partner in dialogue and discourse. The Other is neither vilified nor exoticized. What can we learn here? We can learn from the postmodern questions, insights, and critique, but we as Christ followers will reject the postmodern solution. In the end, the postmodern deconstruction project leaves us with a world in fragments, bereft of meaning or purpose or ways to cooperate and collaborate and converse and make of the world a better human community. No new justice rooted in any reality beyond the community or self has emerged, but only a billion little atoms of individual and communal justice bouncing endlessly and fruitlessly against one another. All that is left is Nietzsche's Dionysian ethic—the ethic of instinct and passion, the "is" with no "ought" to channel it. The one with the most power wins.

I want to make a final framing and balancing comment to avoid confusion: The will to power, pleasure, and fame are not in and of themselves ethically bad or evil. They are natural human instincts or desires. It is when they become self-centered drives that damage other people and other communities that they become distorted and dehumanizing. The most profound ethical commands Jesus gave were to love God with our whole heart and mind and soul and strength, and to love our neighbors as ourselves. Biblically, healthy self-love—the self-love that is the basis for measuring love of neighbor—includes our drive for agency (power), well-being (pleasure), and significance and recognition (fame). The problem, then, is disordered love of self at the center that distorts these drives and makes them destructive in the lives and communities of others. The essence of sin is not "doing bad things" but, in the words of the Anglican confession of sin to God, "we have not loved you with our whole hearts and we have not loved our neighbor as ourselves."[18] The heart of sin is a lack of love. And as Augustine understood so well, idolatry is disordered love, often putting ourselves at the center.[19] We either love God inordinately or, lacking love for God, we love ourselves inordinately.

In the rest of this article, I want to learn what I can from the postmodern critique of Grand Stories and respond to that critique in a way that makes me more deeply and effectively a Christ follower and communicator of the Christian Grand Story.

A Humble Attempt to Reconsider, Recover, and Rejuvenate the Christian Grand Story in Post-Christendom Culture

Here are some crucial questions that the postmodern critique of Grand Stories as expressions of the self-serving will to power presses upon us. How do we more deeply divorce the cross (truth) from the sword (political power) and the dollar (economic power) so that they are not married together in ways that express a self-centered will to power rather than an other-centered offer of forgiveness and freedom? How do we better discern and repent of the unintended injustice in the ways we understand, live, tell, and invite others into the Christian Grand Story? I have suggested the fundamental shift is from a focus on our own social power to a focus on the power of our vulnerability and weakness and suffering in community.

Jesus and Post-Christendom Culture
Jesus believed deeply in truth that was a person and in a true Grand Story. But Jesus radically critiqued the versions of that Grand Story that he encountered in his day and in his culture. I want to suggest that Jesus can be both the model and the message for our renewed and redemptive Christian Grand Story. Jesus had a lot to

18. *Book of Common Prayer*.
19. Augustine, *On Christian Doctrine* I.27.28.

say about Israel's self-serving bias. Israel had come to the point where her very language, institutions, worldview, symbols, and religion were all in cooperation to maintain the dominance and centrality of Israel, and especially male religious Israel, as God's people, and as the eventual winners in the game of history. Jesus confronted every aspect of this ethnocentric, religiously-clothed worldview of Jewish dominance. For religious Jewish men, all others, Gentile, women, the sick, the poor, the lame, the blind, and the sinner, were marginalized, excluded, or devalued. Jesus de-centered Israel but did not devalue Israel. Jesus claimed to fulfill Israel's history and Law and Temple, but also pronounced judgement on the ways idolatry and the will to protect the social power of religious Jewish men had distorted the message and model of Israel to the nations.

The challenge for the Church today is discerning whether or not (and in what degree) we have become like Israel in seeing ourselves at the center, in having a worldview in which we win at the game of history, in which some of us win far more than others of us, and in which all those who are not like us are excluded, dehumanized or devalued. The challenge for us is to pursue Jesus's prophetic ministry of de-centering the Church and the church's version of the Christian Grand Story, in order to enthrone God back in the center, where God actually always ultimately is. In other words, we human beings inevitably use Grand Stories to replace God with ourselves, including our cultural practices, our politics, our economics, our ethnic background and skin color, and our version of Christian faith at the center of our own world, with sometimes explicit and other times implicit claims that it ought to be the center of everyone else's world. Our version of the Christian Grand Story inevitably gets co-opted some by our self-centered will to power. This assertion restates the doctrine of sin in more postmodern terms, but nevertheless in often very accurate terms, long ago hinted at by Isaiah, "All we like sheep have gone astray. We have all turned to our own way" (Isa 53:6). Our version of the Christian Grand Story inevitably becomes distorted, and needs continual correction, renewal, and reformation.

I want to suggest that Jesus becomes the de-centering center for our faith and for our continual pursuit of correcting, renewing, and reforming our version of the Christian Grand Story. Jesus becomes first the critic of our message, model, and methods, and then the catalyst for a corrected, renewed, and reformed message, model, and methods. I am not suggesting that there is no ultimate version of the truth, of the Grand Story of history. But only God can tell the story straight. Since God is the pre-eminent and ultimate subject of the Story, and since God alone is free from the distortions of self-absorbed self-interest, only God can comprehend and communicate that Story without a distorting self-serving will to power. But we are not left therefore in a sea of inescapable relativism. Rather we are called to a continual process of expressing within our cultures the closest approximation of the Christian Grand Story as God has revealed it in Scripture and to the degree that we are able. But we always know that we can never express that Grand Story free from the distorting impact of self-serving bias and the will to power.

And so we must continually subject our message, character, and methods to Jesus. We must return again and again to the Gospels, and to Jesus, not only as our advocate, but also as our critic. Jesus will relate to us just as Jesus related to Israel, radically loving us and radically critiquing us. Again and again, we will discover in and through Jesus the ways we have enthroned ourselves and our own bias and will to power at the center. And so we will be led to repentance and reformation again and again, not only in our character and methods, but even in the way we formulate our message. It is safe to say that the rise of Christian nationalism in the US context is one more version of this "will to power" and "self at the center" of the white evangelical church in America.

Here is just one outstanding example from history. Martin Luther corrected the Catholic Church in some very profound, needed, and powerful ways. The Catholic Church, through its system of indulgences, had replaced God at the center. The church now could dispense forgiveness, a place in heaven, and also raise money and insure its power, all at the same time. Luther critiqued that whole self-serving system and its expression of the will to power, even if not in those terms. Jesus would have done no less. Here cross, sword, and dollar were all intertwined in an oppressive Grand Story that justified corruption and violence.

Luther battled that whole system by recovering the message of God's grace expressed through justification by faith alone through Christ alone. But this powerful and profound message of grace became a new instrument to position the church and the church's ideas at the center instead of God at the center. Grace became the key criterion of who was in and who was out, and in this way, grace became an instrument of exclusion and political warfare. In that sense, the way of the cross was divorced from the message of the cross. So the church could preach the cross, and exclude—often even violently—all those who did not agree. Some followers of Luther then became judgmental, self-righteous, violent, and exclusionary, all in the name of grace!

Jesus decenters an exclusive emphasis on grace that can become weaponized against others. Jesus can never be read in the Gospels as someone who made a fundamental dichotomy between grace and works. Certainly, he rejected the legalism of the Pharisees as a basis for who was in and who was out. But equally, he suggested that the way we treat the poor, and especially those poor who confess Jesus as Lord, will determine how God ultimately judges us. If we received the poor, fed the hungry, clothed the naked, and visited those in prison, we will be with God forever. If we do not, the grace of God has not become effectual in our lives. Matthew 25 (and for that matter the Epistle of James) have never been favorite passages for the descendants of Luther, especially if those descendants have replaced God with their message of grace and, in often subtle ways, with themselves at the center. For Paul, grace always flowed into works. We love because we first have been loved. Grace is prior and preeminent. But grace without works is an illusion, a presumption. As we decenter from our ideas and center on Jesus, our message, character, and methods are renewed. Jesus will always de-center, correct, renew, and reform our version of Jesus and his message and our drive to put ourselves and our culture and our version and vision of church at the center.

A similar analysis applies to evangelical formulations of the message about Jesus, and the methods through which we communicate that message. We, as evangelicals, have emphasized a message of the death of Jesus to pay the price for sins. The goal of salvation is the forgiveness of our sins, so that we can be in relation to God, starting now and going on forever. We will be in heaven. Jesus is the de-centering center for our message and methods as evangelicals. Jesus died and dealt with sin. But Jesus also proclaimed the kingdom or rule of God. The dichotomy between what we believe and how we live and are transformed is an insupportable dichotomy, at least in relation to the message and model and methods of Jesus. Salvation was not just about God's wonderful plan for my own individual life, but even more about God's purpose and plan to redeem and recreate the entire world and cosmos, and to reconcile people, nations and even the larger forces, heavenly and earthly, that keep our world enslaved. Versions that imply that we can "pray a prayer" and be "in" but not be changed are not so very new ways to put ourselves at the center. Cheap grace is no grace at all.

As we continually pursue Jesus as our de-centering center, we will incorporate the true insights of the postmodern (and multi-ethnic) critique of our Grand Stories. But we will not just live in the critique and the deconstruction of our version of Jesus and our ways of living like and talking about Jesus. We will, above all, continually experience the correction, renewal, and reformation of our message, character, and methods. Our primary experience will be of reconstruction and resurrection, not deconstruction. In other words, we invite Jesus and the whole story of Jesus to continually de-center and reform our conceptions of Jesus and our versions of the heart of his story. If we tell the story of Jesus as a story of the forgiveness of sins but not the changing of lives and nations, then our version needs to be corrected and reformed. If our version is mainly about personal piety and not about serving the poor and feeding the hungry, then our version needs to be corrected and reformed. We continually return to the Grand Story of Jesus, and let that story correct and reform our version. Might we need a similar decentering today in the ways we are centering the message on the kingdom of God without fully embracing the character of that kingdom or rule of God as God-initiated and cruciform or cross shaped in character? Without such biblical balance and fullness, a kingdom of God theology can transmute into a triumphalistic human-centered social change campaign.

At the heart of this continual process of renewal through decentering ourselves and our formulations is the embrace of the eschatological lens of the New Testament. Jesus enfleshed and fulfilled the rule of God within history in a way that was unique. The incarnation of God in human flesh, Jesus's proclamation and demonstration through healing and exorcism of the fulfilled rule of God as at hand, the death and resurrection and ascension of Jesus, then the gift of the Spirit, and the eventual return of Jesus must all be understood as "end times" events that can only be understood as God's entering human history in the middle with God's inauguration of what God had promised to do at the end. In Jesus, God judges sin, Satan, and death, God inaugurates the new risen humanity, women and men and the young and the old and people of every ethnic group and nation all dream dreams and see visions and speak truth, God's Spirit collects a harvest from the ends of the earth among all the nations, humanity is judged, and God establishes God's rule finally and fully in the return of Jesus.[20] All these were events at the end of the age. We have a foretaste of God's rule, a down payment in the person of the Holy Spirit, and an experience of the Body of Christ as agent and instrument, pointer, and foretaste to that ultimate reality of God's rule fulfilled on earth as in heaven.[21] The foretaste and pointer toward God's rule is nevertheless always provisional, incomplete, flawed, and limited. All human expression of it, whether among families, churches, justice movements, nations, or renewal movements, are radically compromised by the presence of sin, of this self-centered will to power, pleasure, and fame. Our hope in the future ultimate fulfillment of God's rule relativizes and limits our claims for any present expression. When we can fully embrace a humility about our identity and identifications and ideas, never making them absolute, ultimate, or superior, we will ever be in that posture of receiving critique and renewal from the Scriptures and from our

---

20. For an initial discussion of these events seen through an eschatological lens, see Richardson, *Reimagining Evangelism*, 116–30. For a much more full-orbed discussion, see Wright, *The New Testament and the People of God*, 280–338.

21. Newbigin, *The Household of God*, 128–30.

friends and foes in ways that decenter us from ourselves and lead us back in the direction toward Jesus and the cruciform kingdom of God.

What, then, does evangelism look like practically in the context of relationships with seekers and skeptics today, in light of the postmodern critique about power that echoes the biblical critique of our tendency to always put ourselves at the center? To that question, I want now to turn. This last part of the article will be suggestive, not comprehensive.

Practical Applications for a Post-Christendom Evangelism

Evangelism as Conversations rather than Sales
I want to draw out the implications in relation to a paradigm for evangelism that I have been developing and using on many campuses and also with many churches. The paradigm might be called "evangelism as conversations on a journey." It is an explicit shift from the paradigm that dominated much of twentieth-century evangelism, which might be called, "evangelism as closing the deal on a sales call." I have become convinced that this basic paradigm of evangelism as the practice of individuals seeking to make the close on a sales call permeates the evangelical consciousness, at least up until recently, when it comes to thinking about and pursuing evangelism. It is a paradigm that emphasizes our strength and social power and the superiority of our product and our answers rather than our weakness and our vulnerability and our suffering. There are those who embrace that sales metaphor and constantly update their methods of "winning friends and influencing people." And there are those who reject evangelism altogether in their reaction to this reduced form of sharing the good news. Either way, it centers ourselves as gospel proclaimers and sales people. It teaches us to "win" with the gospel through wise and persuasive methods, minimizing our weakness, vulnerability, and lack of social power. I believe this sales-oriented paradigm emerges out of capitalistic and postmodern performative culture, in which persuasion has become merely sales, focusing on the recipient as the consumer and performativity as the key measure.

Whoever recruits the most contributors and attenders gets the most influence and status.

This paradigm then can be an approach that reinforces the postmodern conclusion that since all truth is merely the expression of the self-serving will to power, then have at it! Express that will to power by "selling" your product to as many people on earth as you can. The one who dies with the biggest consumer base wins! Of course, that conclusion would lead to an unjust caricature of many leaders who developed simple and effective ways to share good news to be used by everyday people in all their spheres of relationship.

Does the paradigm shift I am proposing mean we only talk about journey and not about decision or closure? No. We do have a direction on the journey (toward Jesus), and a destination (to become like Jesus in full union with God). And on the journey, there are crucial turning points (including repentance and faith) and mile markers (including baptism and public identification with Christ and his community). Nevertheless, moving out of the sales paradigm helps us transcend the dangers of "bounded set" thinking, in which we know who is in and who is out, and we reduce salvation to a consumer or at least instrumental transaction, taking out all its mystery as an encounter between people and the Holy Spirit. And it moves us out of the tendency to frame everything in terms of winning.

Does the paradigm shift I am proposing devalue persuasive speech? No. But persuasive speech now fits into a different framework, less susceptible to perceiving persuasive speech as merely advertising and marketing and powering up on people, however subtly. I also want to recognize that many people who have pursued evangelism in these last few decades would claim the biblical book of Acts as their source, and not a Western consumer-oriented paradigm of sales. I do not want merely to draw a caricature of evangelism as sales that is not true to the best examples of twentieth-century evangelistic methods and message. I am just recognizing that contemporary Christians, seekers, and skeptics all need a fresh paradigm in order to re-engage in witness. I also realize that the corrective I am proposing will need its own corrective at some point in the future.

Evangelism as Incorporation into a Conversational Community
Interestingly, on a partially different basis, I find myself pursuing a similar model that Brad Kallenberg pursued in his book, *Live to Tell*.[22] He compares evangelism to teaching a foreign language, because he takes seriously Wittgenstein's insights into the nature of language. We only understand words, and phrases like "the word God," by seeing how that phrase is used in the context of communities and their praxis.[23] Words and propositions only make sense in light of the larger Story and worldview, and what those words do in their context. Evangelism is not just about "passing on words," but rather about incorporating people into a whole language system, community, and worldview. So, I, too, am pursuing a "conversational communities" paradigm for evangelism. What are the characteristics and practices of a conversational-communities approach? Elsewhere I have unpacked some of the key axes of this transformation of evangelism in post-Christendom contexts, including:

- Identifying comes before Influencing[24]
- Experiencing comes before Explaining[25]
- Belonging comes before Believing[26]
- Contributing (as an essential part of belonging) comes before Committing[27]
- Communicating in Image and Sign come before communicating in Words[28]
- Individual and communal narratives of Identity come before metanarratives of Identity
- Vulnerability comes before Verbal Proclamation[29]

22. Kallenberg, *Live to Tell*.
23. Wittgenstein, *The Wittgenstein Reader*, 97–98.
24. Richardson, *You Found Me*, 97–98.
25. Richardson, *Evangelism Outside the Box*, 45–47.
26. Richardson, *Evangelism Outside the Box*, 47–50.
27. Seversen, *Not Done Yet*, 92–105.
28. Richardson, *Evangelism Outside the Box*, 50–51.
29. Richardson, *Reimagining Evangelism*, 22–24.

Here I want to focus on just a few of these implications for an evangelism from the position of vulnerability and social powerlessness within conversational communities.

Practices of Conversational Communities
First, in starting spiritual conversations, do not assume social power and leverage. Instead, assume the need to restore trust. Assume mistrust on the part of seekers and skeptics, identify and validate the mistrust where you can, and then seek healing for the hurt that often lies behind mistrust. I am discovering how easy it is these days to engage people in spiritual conversation. People are very spiritually interested, but they are also very leery of anyone who thinks they know the truth and think that everybody else is wrong. A term often used in our cultural conversations for narrow, doctrinaire, judgmental people is the term fundamentalist. In recent conversations, I have noticed that the term "fundamentalist" has a very specific meaning in people's minds today. To many, fundamentalists have two discerning characteristics: Fundamentalists are people who think they are right and everybody else is wrong; and fundamentalists go around imposing their views assertively, aggressively, and even disrespectfully on others. Fundamentalists can be Christian, Islamic, or atheistic. Frankly, I am just as turned off by the stereotype of fundamentalists as seekers and skeptics are. I am not interested in imposing my views on others, nor having others impose their views on me. And I do not think I am right and everybody else is wrong. I do not have such a dichotomizing nor arrogant mental worldview. I personally do not want to be buttonholed, forced to hear a message I am not interested in, treated like somebody's project, told my opinions and convictions are all wrong, and challenged to join an organization I have never found to be very relevant to my life. Why do I think that I need to do those things *to* seekers and skeptics in the name of Christ? In evangelism, we are to love others as ourselves, just as in every area of life. And the aggressive expression of social power and intellectual arrogance is exactly what people resist and are repelled by.

I therefore can fully identify with and champion the mistrust many people feel toward "absolutists." Of course, I may also want to ask if the person has ever really encountered any of these narrow, judgmental, aggressive, disrespectful people personally. I have found that many people in our culture carry a caricature of fundamentalists that may not be rooted in their own experience but rather in the stereotypes common in the media and in the ways secular critics have told the story of our religious past. My point, though, remains the same. I am finding that starting spiritual conversations is like falling off a log these days. I just need to express some genuine sense of interest in spiritual things, self-deprecation about my own ability to know it all, and also a genuine sense of mistrust or lack of comfortability with "organized religion" and people that think they have all the answers.

Recently, I have had very engaging conversations with five different people who are alienated from the church and from traditional expressions of Christian faith. In each case, I shared some event or experience or project I was working on about how to communicate faith to people who are spiritually interested but turned off by organized religion and by people who think they have all the answers. How do I authentically also keep my commitment to the Christian Grand Story and to Truth? I express positively my commitment to Jesus and the uniqueness of Jesus. For instance, I share that Jesus uniquely in history was God, not giving us a ladder to climb to get to God and become spiritual. Instead, in Jesus, God climbed down the ladder to get us. Then I ask if they need a ladder to climb, or if they need God to climb down the ladder to them. When people ask if I have the immoral and irresponsible belief that only Christians go to heaven and everybody else goes to hell, I tell them, "No!" I do not know what God will do with people who never heard of Jesus. And I do not know what God will do with people who saw only scandal and hypocrisy in the "Christian" people and churches they encountered. I do have a sense that God may hold us who represented Jesus more accountable than those who were pushed away from Jesus.

But I do believe that Jesus is the mystery at the heart of the universe that explains all the other mysteries. And I do believe that Jesus is uniquely the way and the gate and the path to God. I do believe in a God who is God for all people, and in Jesus as the unique and full revealing of that God in human history. And I do believe that people who choose to live alone without God and without hope in this life are choosing to live without God in the next. Through it all, I have come to the conviction that what people are concerned about is not that we affirm some general commitment to relativism, but that we will not judge, exclude, devalue, and even abuse people who think differently than we do. I can remain fully committed to the uniqueness of Jesus as the only way to the Father, but simultaneously break the stereotypes people have about many who hold such convictions. So my goal is to help us recover boldness and clarity in expressing our faith. Many Christians never get past the mistrust they run into when they start to share their faith with others. I am suggesting we can see the mistrust as an opportunity for witness and ministry rather than an insurmountable barrier to witness and ministry. If we combine our confidence in God and God's presence with our sense of our own vulnerability and limits.

Second, as relationships progress, be aware of the power dynamics in those relationships, and seek to change those dynamics when you can. Let me give an example. My family took a vacation to Colorado last summer. We had asked a family to look after our two cats, a dog, and a hamster. They had cheerfully agreed. On the day before we left, we found out that our cat had diabetes and needed shots twice a day. We went to the family that had agreed to watch our animals, told them the situation, and gave them the option to get out of their commitment. They wanted to look after the animals anyway. We returned eight days later deeply grateful and in their debt. Shooting up a cat twice a day is just not the way to have a good time, no matter how you approach it! We were very thankful to this couple. We took them out to a wonderful restaurant for an evening of dining and conversation to express our gratitude. I will never forget the conversation. The man was a police commander, and he and I spent an hour in intense and profound spiritual conversation. He saw his work as a calling, and he believed in God, but could not connect to the organized church. As we shared our stories, we were both challenged and deepened in our spiritual journey with and toward Jesus. That conversation was one of the more powerful and profound conversations I have had in the last few years. He later committed his life to Christ. Later, I reflected on why this man had so opened up to sharing his journey and convictions, and to influencing me and being influenced by me. I realized that the power dynamics in our relationship had positioned me as the vulnerable and grateful recipient of his caring and competency, all because of a diabetic cat.

That experience stimulated me to think about my paradigm of evangelism. I have long believed that I need to care for others and earn the right to be heard. I realized that night that it is sometimes even more powerful, especially in a post-Christendom culture that is very mistrustful about agendas and power and persuasion, to be on the receiving end and in the position of powerlessness. It is sometimes much more trust building for me to ask for help than to always be trying to give help. Asking for advice and insight can be more important than always trying to get in the position of giving advice and insight. It is sometimes far more meaningful for me to share my struggles and weaknesses and failures as a Christ follower with a seeker and skeptic than to share my victories. Do I hear Paul reporting God's still small voice to him in a moment of weakness and vulnerability? "My strength is made perfect in your weakness." The much-quoted step in evangelism of practicing "care evangelism" might be better re-stated: We practice "mutual care evangelism," asking for help as often as we seek to give help. We embrace our vulnerabilities, suffering, and struggles, and find that it is in these postures through which Jesus's power and light shines forth most. Again, the paradigm of evangelism as conversations on a journey is helpful. In the paradigm of evangelism as sales, I have a product that the other person needs, and I am seeking to close the deal on their "purchase" of the product. I come from the power position in the sales model. In the conversations on a journey model, we are more on an equal footing. Which leads us to the next implication.

Third, as you share about Jesus and tell the Story of Jesus, let Jesus continually correct and challenge your seeking and skeptical conversation partner, but let Jesus also continually challenge and correct you. The reality is that we are all seekers somewhere along the journey. There are crucial moments and turning points in that journey, and we will need to emphasize those turning points. But we also accept that the ground on which we all stand is much more level than we had at first thought. We are then free to challenge people boldly with the story and claims of Jesus on their lives, and yet simultaneously be challenged deeply by Jesus through them. It was the found, the righteous, the healthy, and the rich that Jesus constantly seemed to be confronting and challenging when he walked the earth, and presumably still confronts through the Holy Spirit. Often in spiritual conversations with seekers and skeptics, we might find ourselves in the uncomfortable position of learning more and being challenged more than our seeking or skeptical friend. I recently learned this again very deeply through a friendship with a man who has given his life to Christ very recently, but has taught and is teaching me far more than I ever taught him, and is demonstrating a life of prayer and sacrificing for others, both before his conversion and after, that inspires and is changing me. I have also found in my conversations with others that when I talk about the ways in which Jesus upset my views about Jesus, took me down a peg or three, helped me realize my religious wrong turns, people are very engaged. Whenever I share about how Jesus rocked my neat little religious world, people love it and lean in.

I have also been approaching differently the task of training Christians to learn to share their story with seeking and skeptical friends. As I teach people to share their story with seekers and skeptics, I have been teaching them to focus on how Jesus has rocked their world, and how Jesus came into the center of their lives, sometimes replacing even their conceptions of Jesus. I encourage them to focus on their times of struggle, pain, and weakness, and the way God encountered them *in* their weakness, not so as to eradicate weakness but so as to show up in the midst of their weakness and show God's reality. I encourage people to learn to share all such "God showing up in my weakness and pain" stories, not just the first one that led to initial commitment to Christ.

Fourth, cultivate conversational *communities of grace and peace* to which people can belong before they have to believe, contribute before they have committed, and in which people can be invited into whole life transformation and not just belief modification and assent. In other words, become aware of the community dynamics that exclude others and that keep the power and the priorities focused almost solely on believers. Above all, people today will explore faith issues and discover spiritual truth in the context of winsome communities to which people can belong before they have to believe. And belonging includes contributing gifts and time and talent. Most churches are not set up well to be conversational communities where people can enter in, feel welcomed, explore their spiritual commitments and interests, be able to contribute in some way, and try on Christian identity.[30]

Pre-Christendom environments and the corresponding missionary efforts can give us clues about the way forward in post-Christendom contexts, as churches and Christians in both pre- and post-Christendom contexts communicate faith in a situation of relative powerlessness and vulnerability. The missionary efforts outside the Roman empire, starting in Ireland, and then moving through Iona in Scotland to Denmark, Sweden, Finland, and Germany are very instructive. Often in those contexts, missionary brothers and sisters founded abbeys and created conversational communities to which people could belong and contribute before they believed and committed. George Hunter documented some of these kinds of missionary ventures in his "Celtic Way of Evangelism."[31]

When we lack power, and when the people we are trying to engage and with whom we want to communicate do not have the background and experience to even understand what the words we use about God's love and Christ's life and sacrifice and rising mean, we must "proclaim" through providing community that teaches people what the words mean and help people act their way into faith. The early Christian missionary communities did just that, providing a context for people to taste and see, and then come to understand Christian faith and identity and what it looked like and what it meant. They gardened and ate with the brothers or sisters, and then experienced the prayer of the community. There were boundaries too. Eucharist and baptism and leadership were for the committed. But the learners, the catechumens, could help and could see and could try on Christian identity as they participated. The way of the sword was not available to these Christian communities. Only the way of the cross, of suffering service, of

---

30. Seversen, *Not Done Yet*, 25.
31. Hunter, "The Celtic Way for Evangelizing Today," 15–30.

openness and love toward the other. The social powerlessness allows for a spiritual power encounter in which the moral goodness, beauty, depth, and efficacy shine through.[32] These winsome conversational communities have only become that much more urgent for reaching and developing emerging adults in post-Christendom contexts. Emerging adults aged 18–29 are experiencing a period of identity construction and choice, and need to be able to try on Christian identity before committing to Christian identity.[33]

Fifth and finally, embrace and practice hospitality toward the Other—the different, the people not like you.[34] Love those neighbors as yourself. Our greatest need today is not better methods and more creative messaging, though these are still needed. Rather, the greatest need is living a quality of life that is compelling. What we need is love, an unselfconscious Other-focused saintliness of life. Those qualities will never go out of style or fail to speak to every generation, and especially our post-Christendom generations. How does our community enfold the Other, the seeker, the skeptic, the ones who come to our community who are not the norm in our community? And how do we embrace the Other while maintaining our identity and values? The Other can include economic, racial, ethnic, religious, and social Others. How does our community embody its case for faith and case for Jesus? How do we deal with power, with the underdog, with issues of justice, exclusion, and embrace? How do we let the Other influence us even in our identity? How do we make space for the Other, including the adversary and critic, with the goal of embrace? People today are attuned deeply to these questions.

As we become conversational communities that embrace our Others, we will once again discover that witness is not a lost and dying dimension of the Church. It is our lifeblood, and God is at work in our day in mighty and transforming ways. It is not a time to become apologetic in our living, enacting, and telling the Christian Grand Story of Jesus. We may look back and realize the

---

32. Bryan Stone says something similar in Stone, *Evangelism After Christendom*, 12.
33. Seversen, *Not Done Yet*.
34. Pohl, *Making Room*.

opportunity has never been greater or better for living like Jesus and speaking about Jesus. In every culture, post-Christendom culture included, living like Jesus and speaking about Jesus have always been ultimately effectual in history. As Jesus has it, "I will build my church, and not all the gates of hell will prevail against it" (Matt 16:18; paraphrased). Not even death will halt the reach and impact of the gospel through a loving and humble and suffering church.

Practically, then, when I teach and train churches in witness, I am asking people to consider the conversational communities that make up their church or Christian group. Then I encourage them to consider where seekers and skeptics can find relevant and challenging conversation for their stage in the journey. Where can seekers and skeptics connect before they have to commit, belong before they have to believe, and converse about the questions, concerns, values, and beliefs that will guide their lives? What is their entry point into Christian community and Christian conversation?

I am finding that churches and Christian groups begin to get very creative and energized as they pursue the goal of developing conversational community for each stage of the spiritual journey. In many ways, Alpha, seeker small groups, and the recovery movement are all models of conversational communities designed for earlier stages of the spiritual journey. There are many more possible structures for good and challenging conversations, including movie discussions, book clubs, special seeker and skeptic-oriented sermon series, small groups for both believers and the skeptical to talk about Jesus, forums on current issues, involvement in justice and service projects, and so many more. I think, also, the ways we deal with the survivors of sexual abuse and racial bias affect profoundly our witness today. Too often we have protected our institutions and reputations instead of being vulnerable about our mistakes, empathetic to the survivors of sexual abuse and racial discrimination, and then willing to lay down power and prerogatives and put the process of redress, healing, and justice in the hands of those who have been hurt and crushed. When we embrace our own weakness, vulnerability, and blind spots, and yield power to those who have suffered, we will see witness shine forth.

God's power and presence will fill jars of clay and shine out all the brighter for our honesty and authenticity. Recently, I watched a church leadership team live out these practices as a conversational community very beautifully, bringing great healing to survivors of a particularly horrendous situation of abuse at the hands of a leader in the church. The witness of this church shone in the midst of the darkness.

Conclusion

In this paper I have explored the postmodern critique of Grand Stories, owning up to ways that critique has been valid—and sometimes incisively so—about Christendom tendencies to communicate and propagate Christian faith for the purpose of pursuing a self-centered will to power. Signs of church leaders pursuing and expressing a self-centered will toward power while naively claiming the moral and intellectual high ground of absolute truth are especially prominent and problematic in times of social change when the church is losing social power—times like now. Second, I turned to a project of reclaiming the gold of the Christian grand narrative without the dross of a self-centered will to power at its heart. I explored the principle of letting Jesus decenter our politics, practices, and even theological constructs, pointing out ways that the eschatological lens of New Testament fulfillment can give us humility about our limited expressions of truth and ethics within history and within cultures. Finally, I suggested specific applications for how we might proceed in formulating and communicating the Christian metanarrative in a post-Christendom world in which God's power and our weakness, vulnerability, and suffering become intertwined and essential. In particular, I looked at the characteristics of conversational communities of faith that have learned to discern their own self-centered tendencies to pursue the will to power and then, alternatively, I enjoined an embrace of vulnerability, weakness, and suffering combined with a dependence and focus on the presence of Christ as the way forward.

May God give us wisdom as we hear the postmodern, post-Christendom, and multi-ethnic critique of the ways in which we understand and communicate our Grand Story. And may God deepen and strengthen our identity as Christ followers who are on the way to the cross carrying the marks of vulnerability together with the marks of spiritual authority in communicating the Christian Grand Story of Jesus in our post-Christendom culture.

Bibliography

Augustine. *On Christian Doctrine*. Kindle Edition. N.p.: Veritatis Splendor, 2012.

Book of Common Prayer. New York: The Church Hymnal Corporation, N.d. N.p. Online: https://www.bcponline.org.

Crenshaw, Kimberle. "Race, Reform, and Retrenchment: Transformation and Legitimation in Anti-Discrimination Law." In *Critical Race Theory: The Key Writings that Shaped the Movement*, edited by Kimberle Crenshaw et al., 103–25. New York: The New Press, 1995.

Dawn, Marva. *Powers, Weakness and the Tabernacling of God*. Grand Rapids: Eerdmans, 2001.

Derrida, Jacques. *Writing and Difference*. Chicago: University of Chicago Press, 1978.

Emerson, Michael, and Christian Smith. *Divided by Faith: Evangelical Religion and the Problem of Race in America*. New York: Oxford University Press, 2000.

Foucault, Michel. *Power/Knowledge: Selected Interviews and Other Writings*, edited by Colin Gordon. Translated by Colin Gordon, et al. New York: Pantheon, 1980.

Henley, William Ernest. "Invictus." *Poetry Foundation*. N.d. N.p. Online: https://www.poetryfoundation.org/poems/51642/invictus.

Hunter, George. "The Celtic Way for Evangelizing Today." *Journal of the Academy for Evangelism in Theological Education* 13 (1997–1998) 15–30.

Kallenberg, Brad. *Live to Tell: Evangelism for a Postmodern Age*. Grand Rapids: Baker, 2002.

Lyotard, Jean-Francois. *The Postmodern Condition: A Report on Knowledge*. Translated by Geoff Bennington and Brian Masumi. Minneapolis: University of Minnesota Press, 1979.

Newbigin, Lesslie. *The Household of God: Lectures on the Nature of the Church*. London: SCM, 1953.

Nietzsche, Friedrich. *The Portable Nietzsche*, edited and translated by Walter Kaufmann. New York: Penguin, 1954.

Pohl, Christine D. *Making Room: Recovering Hospitality as a Christian Tradition*. Grand Rapids: Eerdmans, 1999.

Richardson, Rick. *Evangelism Outside the Box: New Ways to Help People Experience the Good News*. Downers Grove, IL: IVP, 2000.

———. *Re-Imagining Evangelism: Inviting Friends on a Spiritual Journey*. Downers Grove, IL: IVP, 2006.

———. *You Found Me: New Research on How Unchurched Nones, Millennials, and Irreligious Are Surprisingly Open to Christian Faith*. Downers Grove, IL: IVP, 2019.

Seversen, Beth. *Not Done Yet: Reaching and Keeping Unchurched Emerging Adults*. Downers Grove, IL: IVP, 2020.

Stone, Bryan. *Evangelism after Christendom*. Grand Rapids: Brazos, 2007.

Tisby, Jemar. *The Color of Compromise*. Grand Rapids: Zondervan, 2020.

Volf, Miroslav. *Exclusion and Embrace*. Nashville: Abingdon Press, 1996.

Wittgenstein, Ludwig. *The Wittgenstein Reader*, edited by Anthony Kenny. Oxford: Blackwell, 1994.

Wright, N. T. *The New Testament and the People of God*. Minneapolis: Fortress, 1992.

MODERN AUTHORS INDEX

Amen, D., 37
Ansgar of Bremen, 3, 5, 14–18
Arndt, J., 20

Bainton, R., 6, 9, 11, 12
Baker, P., 64–66
Balmer, J., 13, 14
Barth, K., 43–45, 61
Bass, D. B., 60
Berger, P., 34, 41
Berjeau, J. P., 16
Bettenson, H., 6, 9, 21
Bloom, A., 35
Boghossian, P., 44
Bosch, D. J., 60, 61, 63
Bunkowske, E. W., 57
Burger, D. T., 24, 25
Brad, M., 37

Campbell, J., 24–26
Carr, N. G., 37
Carson, D. A., 5
Chadwick, H., 7
Choung, J., 26
Clark, E., 14
Collins, F., 44
Connaughton, A., 39
Constantine, 6

Cooper, B., 38, 39
Cox, D., 60
Crenshaw, K., 86
Cullhed, S. S., 14

Davidson, R., 38
Dawn, M., 83
DeJong, A., 33
Deneen, P. J., 44
Derrida, J., 85
Dickson, J., 9
Doberstein, J. W., 58, 59
Douglas, M., 35
Drucker, P., 48

Elert, W., 56, 57
Ellingsen, M., 34, 48
Emerson, M., 84
Engelsviken, T., 62

Ferguson, E., 9, 12, 13
Feuerbach, L., 42
Finney, J., 11–13
Foucault, M., 82, 84
Francke, A., 3, 5, 18–21, 26, 58
Freeman, P., 10
Frei, H., 40–41, 43, 46
Freud, S., 36

Giberson, K., 44
Guder, D. L., 26, 61
Gustafson, D. M., 12

Hamilton, A., 35
Hartenstein, K., 61–62
Hatch, D., 14
Hawking, S., 44–45
Heesen, A., 15
Hempton, D., 23
Hendrix, S. H., 57
Henley, W. E., 80–81
Herder, J. G., 35
Holland, T., 8
Humphreys, H. N., 15, 16
Hunter, G. G., 10, 11, 13, 102

Immordino-Yang, M. H., 37

James, F. A., 18, 19, 22
Jenson, R. W., 45–46
Jeyaraj, D., 58
Jones, R. P., 60

Kaiser, W. C., 63
Kallenberg, B., 96
Kant, I., 35
Kolb, R., 56–58
Kreider, A., 7
Kreider, E., 7
Kuhn, T., 45

Legge, M. J., 67
Lehmann, M. E., 68
Licinius, 6
Liefeld, W. L., 14
Lindbeck, G., 43, 46

Lipka, M., 33, 38, 39
Luther, M., 56–57, 69, 90–91
Lyotard, J., 76, 82

Madison, J., 35
Malpica-Padilla, R., 66–67, 70
Mansfield, S., 11
Marshall, C. T., 11
Martin, F., 22
Maunder, C., 6, 9
McCall, M., 22
McGavran, D., 63
Melin, P. B., 15
Mercadante, L., 34, 39
Muhlenberg, H. M., 58–59
Murray, S., 3

Nasmith, D., 3, 5, 23–26
Newberg, A., 38
Newbigin, L., 26, 59, 93
Nietzche, F., 80–82, 87
Nommensen, L., 68

Öberg, C. S., 15
Öberg, I., 56
O'Brien, P., 64–65
O'Loughlin, T., 10–12
Olsen, R. E., 18

Patterson, J. A., 6
Perkins, J., 26
Peterson, C. M., 71
Plütschau, H., 58
Pohl, C. D., 103
Proba of Rome, 3, 5, 13–14
Protten, R., 3, 5, 22–23, 26

Reid, T., 36
Richardson, R., 93, 96
Rimbert, 14
Robert, D., 6, 7
Rousseau, P., 8
Rudnick, M. L., 6, 7

Sattler, G. R., 19–22
Schaff, P., 10, 13
Scharpff, P., 18–21, 24
Scherer, J. A., 56, 57
Schreiter, R. J., 66
Sensbach, J. F., 22–24
Seversen, B., 96, 102, 103
Shantz, D., 58
Shaw, I. J., 24
Sheridan, M., 7
Small, G. W., 37
Smietana, B., 38
Smith, C., 84
Smith, D., 64
Smither, E. L., 8
Sosnik, D. B., 36
Spener, P. J., 19
Stark, R., 7, 8, 9
Stoeffler, F. E., 58
Stone, B., 3, 103

Tappert, T. G., 58, 59
Taylor, C., 34
Taylor, M., 19–21
Thiessen, J., 33

Tholuck, A., 19, 21
Tisby, J., 84
Tucker, R., 15
Tuttle, R. G., 13, 14
Twenge, J., 48

Van Gelder, C., 59, 61
Van Neste, R., 56, 57
Volf, M., 78–80, 82
Volz, C. A., 16
Vretemark, M., 15

Warneck, G., 56–57
Warren, R., 48
Weber, J., 39, 42
White, J. E., 34
Wilkins-LaFlamme, S., 33
Williams, R., 61
Wilson, E. O., 44
Wilson, S. H., 58
Wimber, J., 26
Winroth, A., 15
Winn, C. T. C., 18
Wittgenstein, L., 80, 96
Woodbridge, J. D., 18, 19, 22
Wright, N. T., 93

Zeigenbalg, B., 58
Zscheile, D. J., 61
Zuckerman, P., 42

www.ingramcontent.com/pod-product-compliance
Lightning Source LLC
Chambersburg PA
CBHW070933160426
43193CB00011B/1677